GOETHE

SELECTED POEMS

EDITED WITH INTRODUCTION,
NOTES & BIBLIOGRAPHY BY
T.J. REED

PUBLISHED BY BRISTOL CLASSICAL PRESS
GENERAL EDITOR: JOHN H. BETTS
GERMAN TEXTS SERIES EDITOR: PETER HUTCHINSON

First published in 1999 by
Bristol Classical Press
an imprint of
Gerald Duckworth & Co. Ltd
61 Frith Street
London W1V 5TA
e-mail: inquiries@duckworth-publishers.co.uk
Website: www.ducknet.co.uk

Reprinted 2000

A catalogue record for this book is available
from the British Library

ISBN 1-85399-592-4

Printed in Great Britain by
Booksprint

CONTENTS

Goethe: Life Dates

(Dates of the major collections and editions of Goethe's poems are in bold type.)

1749	Johann Wolfgang Goethe born on 28 August in the Free Imperial City of Frankfurt am Main, to Catharina Elisabeth (née Textor) and Johann Caspar, well-off bourgeois patricians.
1752-65	Educated by private tutors.
1756-63	Seven Years War.
1765-8	Student of Law in Leipzig. Writes imitative Rococo verse.
1768	Returns home ill. Involvement with a Pietist group.
1770-1	Student in Strasburg. Friendship with Herder. Romance with Friederike Brion at Sesenheim. Reads Shakespeare, Ossian, Homer, Pindar. First poems in his own voice.
1771-4	Works as lawyer in Frankfurt and Wetzlar. Writes the historical play *Götz von Berlichingen*, many of his great early poems, and the sensational novel *Die Leiden des jungen Werthers*. Also at some time in these years, not precisely dateable, begins work on *Faust*.
1775	Uneasy engagement to Lili Schönemann. Escapes to Switzerland. *November*: arrival in Weimar.
1776-86	Works in the Weimar administration and becomes friends with Duke Carl August. Practical tasks supervising roads, forests and mines stimulate scientific interests: geology, botany, meteorology, anatomy, later optics and colour theory. Organises the Weimar theatre. Also a kind of court poet. Intense but unclear emotional relationship with a court lady, Charlotte von Stein.
1778	First (manuscript) collection of the poems.
1786	Increasingly frustrated by relations with Charlotte, by administrative burdens, and by lack of time for larger literary projects – *Faust*, the novel *Wilhelm Meister*, and a good handful of other works. *September*: flight to Italy; a sense of release and rebirth.
1786-8	Based in Rome; travels to Naples, Sicily. Intensive study of art and ancient remains. Writes hardly any poetry; busy revising and completing earlier works for first collected edition: *Iphigenie auf*

	Tauris, Egmont, Torquato Tasso; some further scenes for *Faust*, soon to be abandoned and published in the eight-volume *Schriften* as a fragment.
1788	*June*: back in Weimar. Takes Christiane Vulpius as mistress (marries her in 1806).
	September: first of the *Römische Elegien*.
1789	Birth of August, their only child to survive. Revolution in France.
1789	First published collection of Goethe's poems under the title *Vermischte Gedichte*, the last volume (of eight) in the edition *Goethes Schriften*, published by Göschen in Leipzig.
1790	A second but disillusioning Italian journey, to Venice.
1792	Accompanies Carl August on the German princes' disastrous incursion into France, aimed at reversing the Revolution and restoring the Bourbon monarchy.
1794	*August*: beginning of friendship and literary partnership with the dramatist and aesthetic theorist Friedrich Schiller.
1794-1805	The decade of Weimar Classicism, immensely fruitful for both men in poetry, drama, narrative and theoretical works. Goethe: *Wilhelm Meisters Lehrjahre*, the rest of *Faust I*, *Hermann und Dorothea*, elegies, scientific work; Schiller: *Wallenstein, Maria Stuart, Die Jungfrau von Orleans, Wilhelm Tell*, major aesthetic and critical essays. Jointly: ballads, satirical epigrams. Weimar becomes the most authoritative centre of German literary culture since the Middle Ages – a status contested, however, both by older writers and by the rising generation of the Romantics.
1800	The seventh and last volume of the edition *Goethes neue Schriften*, published by Unger in Berlin from 1792 on, contains most of the poems written in the decade since the *Schriften*, arranged on a new principle of division into lyrical sub-genres – songs, ballads, elegies, epigrams, etc.
1805	Death of Schiller. Goethe ill and depressed.
1806	Prussians defeated by Napoleon at Jena.
1806	The 13-volume edition *Goethes Werke*, is brought out by Cotta in Stuttgart (henceforward Goethe's regular publisher) between 1806 and 1810. It brings together almost all Goethe's poetry from 1770 to date, with the poems for the first time taking pride of place in volume 1 in 1806. Tension shows between the principles of arrangement on biographical or thematic, 'subjective' or 'objective' grounds.
1808	Publishes *Faust* Part I.
1808	Meets Napoleon.

1809	Begins writing the autobiography of his early years, *Dichtung und Wahrheit*.
1814-18	Poems of the *West-östlicher Divan*. A new love, Marianne Wille-mer.
1813	Napoleon's failed Russian campaign.
1815	Battle of Waterloo and end of Napoleon's career.
1815	*Goethes Werke*, in thirteen volumes, with the bulk of the poems now taking up two volumes, and yet others scattered through the edition.
1816	Death of Christiane.
1816-18	Publishes *Italienische Reise*.
1821	First version of *Wilhelm Meisters Wanderjahre*.
1825-31	Work on *Faust* Part II.
1827	A further edition of *Goethes Werke* is begun, the 'Vollständige Ausgabe letzter Hand' in which Goethe tries to give his life's work the shape in which he wants posterity to see it.
1832	Death of Goethe on 22 March.

For Francis Lamport

INTRODUCTION

1

Reading Goethe's poems means coming at a writer of immense and potentially overawing stature at the point where he is most accessible – most open in his account of personal experience, his enthusiasms, commitments, quandaries, insights, ideas; and most comprehensible in the language he uses to convey these things. His poems are rarely difficult, scarcely ever abstruse. They may arise from private occasions, but he writes always in open code, in the common language: 'Ich sah dich'; 'Du gingst, ich stund'; 'Kennst du das Land?', 'Du hast gut reden'; 'Und nun bist du gar nicht da'. The words could not be more simple, more conversational even. They hardly seem 'poetic', yet in context they become powerful bearers of feeling. Other phrases that are brilliantly innovative, cutting through convention to capture an insight or emotion, often at the very start of a poem – 'Wie im Morgenrot/ Du rings mich anglühst', 'Fetter grüne, du Laub', 'Warum gabst du uns die tiefen Blicke?' – create the illusion of ordinary speech because they too keep to the simplest everyday structures and sound almost like something that might be said in casual conversation. Indeed, all these quotations are direct address to a 'du' – in context, to many different kinds of 'du' – whose presence, real or imagined or wished for, gives the poem its first impetus. Goethe famously called all his works fragments of a great confession, 'Bruchstücke einer großen Konfession',[1] and that applies as much to the language as to the content of what he says. A confession has to speak plainly if it is really to be one.

This may seem an obvious thing to say about a modern poet. The nineteenth century is full of highly individual voices speaking about themselves, and we still assume (some twentieth-century appearances and theories to the contrary) that lyrical poetry is personal communication. But it took a historic turn to make it so, and Goethe was earliest and foremost among the handful of eighteenth-century European writers who brought it about. Yet even a major turn may virtually disappear from view once it has become a settled assumption. Reading Goethe's poems allows us, among other pleasures, to relive the historic turn and be in at the forming of that assumption.

To stress the accessibility of Goethe's poetry is not to suggest that the rest of his writing is inaccessible. His novels and dramas have the same qualities writ large. From the exploration of private experience in the poetry he moves outward to the understanding of other minds and hearts in more complex human interactions. His language in these less directly personal modes has a similar intensity. *Die Leiden des jungen Werthers* is written in a highly charged, often poetic prose that wrings the last drop of pathos from its subject and was certainly a factor in making the novel a European sensation. *Faust*, the central work of Goethe's creative life, is as much a poetic text as it is a drama, illustrating in its twelve thousand lines more or less every kind of thing that can be done in and with verse in German. All this makes the poetry an ideal base for the reader too to move outward from and explore Goethe's whole work.

But above all the poetry is a rewarding place to be for its own sake. Or rather, it is a great many places and a great many occasions, each memorably rendered, overall a sampling of experience that embodies what lyrical poetry does best. Where narrative stands back to record a succession of events as if they took place in the past, and where drama stages conflict and resolution as if they were happening before our eyes in the real present, a lyrical poem takes a single moment out of time to plumb the perceptions and responses that were concentrated in it. The word 'moment' is deceptive. Given the intricacies of the inner life, it can take far more than a brief poem to unfold the perceptions and emotions that are packed into the briefest span of time: beauty, love and loss, happiness and despair, hopes and memories, and sometimes a glimpse of the pattern these things compose.

Few poets have captured as many such moments as Goethe, if only because he lived longer than most, and few poets have captured them with such consistent quality from start to finish. There are few juvenilia. Almost from the outset Goethe's poetry is original, new in the personal immediacy of what he is saying, new in the ways he finds to say it. It is also mature from early on – as poetry, that is, which means not a precocious personal maturity but a precocious ability to express immaturity fully in all its moods: excitement, love, rebellion, aspiration. Equally, there are no senilia. Goethe's lyrical writing never flagged or went flat. He did not, as may happen to a poet with advancing years (think of Wordsworth), outlive his own genius. He renews himself repeatedly with fresh starts in different styles and cultural guises, although behind them all – Classical, Persian, Chinese – the voice stays familiar. ('Jeder Geist hat seinen Klang', wrote Nietzsche.) Old age does not lessen the expressive power, it simply alters the perspective. The changed emotions of later life are a challenge. Subtler means have to be found to express the poignancy of ageing and the loss of the more obviously lyrical impulses that are so vigorously present in his earlier years. Yet age is also a resource, because a lifetime's experience can give resonance to the simplest statement. It can echo earlier events, earlier loves, earlier poems. The writer becomes in some measure his own tradition, his own source of intertextual richness.

There is nothing self-centred, in the disapproving sense of the word, about this relation with the history of his developing self. From early on Goethe was aware that what he was living through and feeling could also stand for wider human experience: 'Sie wissen, wie symbolisch mein Dasein ist', he wrote to Charlotte von Stein in December 1777. The self he was exploring just happened to be his, nearest to hand and easiest to observe. A sense of shared experience – it is not too much to say: of human solidarity – made communication both possible and necessary. Goethe knew from early experience that it worked from the other direction, from his predecessors to himself. He embraced poets and thinkers of the past, most notably Homer, Pindar, Lucretius, Shakespeare, Ossian, Spinoza, with an enthusiasm that was untouched by the rivalry or envy writers are alleged always to feel, and sometimes do. They and he were part of a single continuing system of interpersonal communication. The writer drew from the common heritage and himself added to it.

Past writers and thinkers moreover were only the pinnacles of a still wider human community. In a letter to two theologian friends, the young Goethe asserts his own experience as something valid in itself and not in need of any authorising by theologians: 'Brauch ich Zeugnis, daß ich bin? Zeugnis, daß ich fühle?'[2] What he did need, and the letter says it is something he esteems, loves and reverences, was the record other human beings had left of experiences matching and confirming his own – 'wie tausende oder einer vor mir eben das gefühlt haben, das mich kräftiget und stärket'. 'Das Wort der Menschen' was for him 'Wort Gottes', whether it came down to us from priests or prostitutes, as a formal canon or as a scatter of fragments. The afterthought 'oder einer' is telling: it only takes one other human being to make a community of experience.

So wherever in Goethe's life we sample his poems, they can be read as highly personal statements and also as invitations to general assent: isn't this how it feels, what life is like, what we human beings are? His personal responses are not exclusive but exemplary. The exulting cry 'Wie herrlich leuchtet mir die Natur!' marks a moment of delight, but also offers an example of how the world can be seen and felt – offers, in other words, not something rich and strange, but something that must have been experienced by multitudes of human beings for whom the poet articulates what they could not express.

Sometimes, especially after the Italian journey, from which he believed he had brought back vital and permanent truths, Goethe's exemplariness can have a didactic ring – 'this is how life *should* be lived'. But the prescription is meant to be liberating, not limiting. At the centre of his Classical vision are the *Roman Elegies* with their attempt to relive Antiquity, their domesticated pagan ideal of a way of love that is still possible – sensuous and spontaneous, warm and generous, free from the self-tormenting conscience of Christian modernity. That example, in a still Christian and highly conventional society, was a conscious provocation. Finally, the poetry of Goethe's last years is exemplary in its acceptance of an autumn when the world is seen with detachment, its patterns recognised, yet its every detail still felt with a calm intensity. Many of Goethe's poems are thus archetypes of a given stage in human growth, and together they make up a coherent record of that entire process. If this sounds a bit too orderly, a time for everything and everything in its time, there can be archetypal disorder too. The very old Goethe is shattered as never before by falling in love again. He is seventy-four, she is eighteen, no good can possibly come of it – except one of his greatest poems, a raw and dark elegy which he then has to struggle to contain, like some piece of radioactive material, in a carefully constructed sequence, the *Trilogie der Leidenschaft*.

This emphasis on archetypal episodes is not an invitation to read Goethe's poems as biographical documents in the way nineteenth-century scholars sometimes did. Yet it does make sense to read them connectedly and cumulatively rather than in isolation, to see them as the products of a single sensibility that shows consistencies beneath variety and change, or (to put it the other way round) plays variations on basic perceptions and ideas. For example, *Maifest* was written when Goethe was twenty-two, *Wenn im Unendlichen* when he was seventy-eight, but they share a strikingly similar vision. In both, natural phenomena are integrated in a general pattern, intense delight in particular things combines with the perception – it is not any kind of doctrinal belief, but an intense intuition – that a benevolent force holds them together and can be felt through them. Things are in constant motion, but within a stable and coherent order. Indeed the constant motion actually constitutes that order; nature is not an assemblage of objects but an active force, *natura naturans*. It is this dynamic order that is most deeply satisfying to experience and contemplate.

In the half-century between those two poems, the perspective has changed from that of a young man intoxicated with the sights and sounds of the Alsace countryside to that of an old man eavesdropping the workings of the universe. In his twenties he is too caught up in excitement and activity to feel it all composing a paradoxical 'ewige Ruh in Gott dem Herrn', yet he does already intuit love as a universal cohesive force in the world around him. In his seventies he no longer has such avid senses to divert his cosmic imagination, yet he can still feel the 'Lebenslust' that streams out of all phenomena. The structure of his vision of reality, and correspondingly of the poetic text, stays constant. That is not primarily a matter of biography, even if it was the young man's enthusiasm for the natural world that later fuelled a lifelong study of science, of which the old man's visionary poem reaps the harvest. The empirical life that can be documented and narrated is only the outward connection between these widely scattered creative moments. The essential connection is the set of mind and imagination within the biographical being, what *Dauer im Wechsel* calls 'den Gehalt in deinem Busen und die Form in deinem Geist'. The poem's last line asserts this distinctive personal pattern of feeling and form as the one constant thing in a world of flux and the one possible survivor beyond the individual's physical life. And it is this pattern that responds to life's occasions to create a lyrical life's work.

2

Responding to occasions is the essence of Goethe's poetry and ultimately of the historic turn sketched above. 'Alle meine Gedichte sind Gelegenheits-gedichte, sie sind durch die Wirklichkeit angeregt und haben darin Grund und Boden', he told Eckermann (18 September 1823). 'Gelegenheitsgedicht' was an old term, but it had always before meant poems celebrating public occasions such as victories, dynastic marriages, births and deaths, poems commissioned by the great, or at least the elevated bourgeoisie, on whom poets commonly depended for patronage.[3] For a poet to treat the occasions of private life just as seriously presupposed economic but also intellectual independence, a leap of the imagination, above all the confidence to assume that his private occasions could be of general interest. There was surely a powerful logic behind such an assumption. The claim of everyday occasions on readers' interest was stronger and closer to home than that of the public events in which they shared, at best, only as a faceless collective, a conformist congregation, a gawping crowd. In contrast, the vicissitudes of everyday life were in some form everyone's experience. There was something to sympa-thise, even to identify with.

There had of course been poems on non-public themes before Goethe, poems of love, mourning, reflection, nature-description; but in all these the poet had worked under constraints. Love poems came in long-established forms: idyll and elegy, anacreontic dalliance and ritual Petrarchan resigna-tion. There was limited scope for the direct expression of present feeling. Among Goethe's predecessors, only Johann Christian Günther sometimes achieves it, and of his older contemporaries only Friedrich Gottlieb Klop-stock. But Klopstock was an intensely Christian poet. Even in an overtly love poem he may be found buttonholing God and trying to place the lovers' destiny in a providential pattern.[4] Other areas of experience were inseparable from Christian thinking. Affliction and mourning had to fit into the framework of theodicy, the doctrine that suffering and loss must be for the best; if human eyes could not see how that was so, it only proved the divine intelligence could. It was hard for any aspect of the inner life to be expressed without reference to divine purpose. Indeed the 'inner life' as such was very largely a Christian invention and monopoly. True, the forms Christianity created would later be a resource for secular poetry, as in Goethe's first *Wandrers Nachtlied*; but that was no part of the intention. The Christian monopoly embraced nature poems too. Poets might record earthly phenomena lovingly and with minute attention, as Barthold Hinrich Brockes does in multiple volumes; but the poem always had to end by proving and praising the divine benevolence and ingenuity. Hence the paradoxical title of Brockes' collections, *Irdisches Vergnügen in Gott*. What now reads as a charming naïvety was the product of ideological constraint.

In these social and intellectual circumstances, it was a revolutionary act when Goethe took the stuff of ordinary experience that was under his nose, and wrote about it in an idiom shaped by current non-rhetorical speech. It was scarcely a conscious programme; rather, he did it by following his pen. He was writing strongly characteristic idiomatic language in his letters as early as the 1760s, at a time when his poetry was still caught in the daisy-chains of anacreontic fashion. He will hardly have been much helped by the European letter-novel of Rousseau and Richardson, with its high artificiality of style. One can only speculate about an early and lasting effect of his mother's vigorous temperament and colourful forthright speech, as preserved in her delightful letters.[5] But whatever early influences made him the person he was, Goethe's poetry is the result of being himself.

That was the more possible, if still not easy, thanks to the German Enlightenment, which for decades had been striving to free the individual from all kinds of imposed conformity that might block human fulfilment. Such conformity, so Kant argued in a celebrated essay defining Enlightenment[6] was in a sense *self*-imposed: nobody *had* to let a way of thinking be imposed on them once they had come of age, and coming of age was a necessary stage in everyone's growth. So it was only cowardice and laziness, Kant argued, that prevented them from exercising the natural rights of their maturity. But this was to ignore the absolutist power of princes who ruled the many separate states composing eighteenth-century Germany, and were answerable to nobody in the exercise of that power. Any licence to free discussion within their states was at best provisional and could be withdrawn at the drop of a hat, or of a crown. Frederick the Great of Prussia prided himself on being 'enlightened', and positively encouraged the open criticism of religion, but his devout successor re-imposed strict orthodoxy. Even Frederick would have frowned on serious discussion of political questions. Still, the aim of Enlightenment writers remained to widen the scope of individual freedom by 'Salamitaktik' while reassuring rulers that no risk attached to open communication within society on matters of common concern.

These are values that Goethe grew up with and internalised, though they must have been intertwined with the elements of a conventional religious upbringing. There are clear Enlightenment elements in his work, especially in the struggles of reflective individuals – Werther, Iphigenie, Torquato Tasso – against an obdurate social code. Presenting such struggles in a narrative or drama, and setting them in real societies and situations, brought the principle home more powerfully than abstract philosophical statement ever could. The individualism Goethe's poetry embodies makes the principle more concrete still, and takes it a vital step further. For the Enlightenment's efforts on behalf of the individual were essentially negative, aimed at undoing constraints and achieving what Georg Simmel called an 'Individualismus der Freiheit'. But what would this leave individual human beings free *for*, free to do and to be? There had to be a positive conception to fill the gap. The answer surely was, to become their distinctive selves and realise a potential that was bound to differ widely from one to another: in Simmel's complementary phrase, an 'Individualismus der Einzigkeit'.[7] Poetry could set an example of how people might have not just the courage of their convictions but the courage of their uniqueness. Looking back, at the very end of his life, Goethe thought he could claim to have done just that, taught Germans generally and poets in particular to live in accordance with their inmost selves – 'von innen heraus leben.' It entitled him to call himself their liberator: 'so darf ich mich wohl ihren Befreier nennen.'[8] He is thinking not primarily, perhaps not at all of politics. His example is nonetheless of fundamental significance for a liberal society.

To say that Goethe's poems show a representative human being, but also that poems are a medium for expressing endless individual human differences, is not the contradiction it may seem at first sight. Human differences exist within a general similarity, as variations on a theme. Whether we perceive divergence or kinship is a matter of the level, or the organ of perception. People *know* they are alike, but *feel* they are different, and of the two, feeling is the more powerful. Goethe put it in an epigram as early as 1785:

> Alle gleichen wir uns, denn wir sind eines Geschlechtes;
> Allen gleichen wir nicht, sagt einem jeden das Herz.

So if there is no necessary contradiction between difference and community, there is certainly a gap for poetry to bridge. It has to find ways to make people *feel* they are alike. To do that, it has to make clear the common ground, make it clear and make it real. That means formulating personal experience in such a way that the reader can enter into it, not merely know it from without. It must generate not just sympathy, which still keeps some distance, but empathy, 'Einfühlung'. The concept was coined by Herder to mean precisely that process of feeling your way into alien experience which is required if other persons (to say nothing of other cultures) are to be fully understood.

Empathy, like almost everything else in Goethe's conceptual world, is dynamic. It involves movement beyond the reader-self's usual limits into someone else's mental and emotional realm. Goethe's poems take the initiative in this. They scarcely wait to be approached, but positively draw us in by some of the most direct openings to be found in poetry anywhere. There is no rhetorical throat-clearing, no preparatory pumping of the bellows to work up an emotional temperature. The poem goes straight into its theme, which usually means straight into the specific situation and the speaker's response, both of them often physical, which grips the attention even more. That is part of the revolution of his early poems: 'Mir schlug das Herz, geschwind zu Pferde'; 'Wie herrlich leuchtet mir die Natur'; 'Bedecke deinen Himmel Zeus'; 'Spude dich, Kronos, Fort den rasselnden Trott'; 'Ich saug an meiner Nabelschnur Nun Nahrung aus der Welt'; 'Meine Ruh ist hin, mein Herz ist schwer'; 'Warum ziehst du mich unwiderstehlich Ach in jene Pracht?'. At the end of his life he is still operating in the same way: ''Dämmrung senkte sich von oben'; 'Was soll ich nun vom Wiedersehen hoffen?'; 'Im ernsten Beinhaus war's'; 'Willst du mich sogleich verlassen?'. Few of his openings are any sort of grand fanfare. Even Prometheus' defiant address to Zeus, or the passenger's imperious command to his coachman in *An Schwager Kronos*, is not grand poetic gesture but flows from the dramatic situation. And once drawn in, we follow a critical path that is hard to miss through a structure of syntax and meaning that is largely self-explanatory. There is little purely private reference such as might block communication. Instead, significantly, even the small adjustments Goethe made in the course of the poem's genetic and printing history are calculated to smooth the way for fuller empathy. Deleting the details of time and place which originally made some of the early poems seem like diary-entries already edges private utterance towards general statement. *An Schwager Kronos* loses its date, *Ich saug an meiner Nabelschnur* (which was actually written in a diary) loses its date and place and becomes *Auf dem See*. Similarly *Im Herbst 1775* is retitled *Herbstgefühl*. Real occasions were essential for the poems' genesis, but once created the poems no longer need the support of a specific location in time and place and in the individual life. They have become free-standing evocations, *An Schwager Kronos* of journeying and ambition and life felt as heroic fulfilment, *Auf dem See* of the way balance and self-confidence are restored by an unspoiled world, *Herbstgefühl* of the rootedness of love, pains and all, in organic nature. The originating occasion has done its work, but something specific has become something general. That does not mean it is now vague or abstract or impersonal, rather it is trans- or interpersonal, a middle stage that can mediate between individualities. Readers, Goethe wrote, can take over what was once peculiar to him into their own peculiar selves and situations.[9] It is a classically simple model of how communication works. If it seems almost naïvely simple, that is because of a modern prejudice that all communication is difficult if not impossible, and that only writing that is difficult can be culturally serious. But such prejudice is just a different and infinitely more damaging naïvety.

When Goethe wrote the words just quoted, he was actually objecting to the practice of readers who failed to accept the poem as an achieved general expression and instead pried into the 'ultra-specific' circumstances ('die Spezialissima') from which it had arisen. Such curiosity put the creative process into reverse and crudely undid the poet's work. Things were different, however, if Goethe judged that he had not turned private experience sufficiently into general statement for others to grasp and assimilate it. He was then prepared to fill in the 'allerbesondersten Umstände' ('die Spezialissima' again, in German guise) that had been the poem's originating occasion. He wrote, for example, a detailed commentary on the poem *Harzreise im Winter* as a direct response, which is itself part of the communicative system, to the difficulties a commentator had plainly had with it. He wrote similar commentaries on poems that offered technical problems, philosophical in *Urworte. Orphisch*, scientific in a poem celebrating the English meteorologist Luke Howard. In doing this, he was aware of the risk that poetry might be reduced to prose, but ready to take that risk in the interests of poetic understanding. On a larger scale, the hundred-and-fifty pages of notes and essays that he appended to his collection of poems in the Persian style – *Noten und Abhandlungen zu besserem Verständnis des West-Östlichen Divans* – are a very concrete recognition that readers may need help and context and a greater measure of relevant knowledge than the poem can always itself contain, if they are to get to its essential 'general sense'. And on a larger scale still, the account of his youth in *Dichtung und Wahrheit*, and the other autobiographical writings that covered later parts of his career, were meant as a personal and historical framework for the fuller understanding of his works. For these 'fragments of a great confession', in a proper reading of that statement, were as much fragments as confession. Something was needed to join them up and make his life's work more than the sum of its parts. Thus at every stage, from the language of the individual line via the help he gave towards understanding the rare difficult poem, on through the annotation of a culturally alien work and right up to the broad historical picture of the forces that shaped him and his oeuvre – in all these steadily widening contexts Goethe is committed to communication.

It is consistent with Goethe's communicative impulse that anything which seemed wholly private was left not just unexplained but unpublished. The poem *Warum gabst du uns die tiefen Blicke* is not wholly self-explanatory from within the text. It requires a knowledge of 'die allerbesondersten Umstände' of Goethe's relationship with Charlotte von Stein, knowledge that scarcely anyone possessed in Goethe's lifetime and that he would not willingly have supplied, for the sake of his and her privacy. Time has supplied it. But the delay was beneficial. With what we now know, we can read the poem not just as a document of their joint biographies but as the expression of an emotional and intellectual situation which, bizarre as it is, becomes part of the poetic record of possible human experience. Time and distance have made the poem, for all its specificity and strangeness, into a kind of general statement.

3

One more thing that follows from a poetry of occasions is a kind of realism, out of place though that term may seem in discussions of poetry. For each occasion was composed of a particular set of real circumstances that chance had brought together. That is half the meaning of 'Erlebnislyrik', a term traditionally applied to Goethe's poetry but often misunderstood as meaning merely that the poem it labels was the product of private emotion. That is to leave out the world. 'Erlebnis', each separate experience, is inherently dual, a meeting of the individual sensibility with external things, an occurrence in the real world. In exploring himself, the poet is exploring the world he lives in too. Goethe does this graphically. The sights of a ride through the dusk in *Willkommen und Abschied*, the brightness of morning light and mood on the water in *Auf dem See*, the still-life landscape of *Über allen Gipfeln*, the stones of Rome's public spaces and the lovers' secluded room with its blazing fire in the *Römische Elegien* – these and other images imprint themselves on the memory. No one's poems are more concrete, so rarely abstract. What makes their images so live is that they are often moving, in the literal sense, evoking and narrating physical movement. The poetic speaker moves through landscapes – the dusk ride again, the muddy march through the storm in *Wandrers Sturmlied*, the coach ride in *An Schwager Kronos*, the trepid-intrepid skater

in *Eis-Lebens Lied*, the seafarer in *Seefahrt*. Goethe's poems were often
stimulated by bodily movement, by walking, riding, swimming, travelling.
He was well aware of the link: 'Was ich Gutes finde in Überlegungen,
Gedanken, ja sogar Ausdruck, kommt mir meist im Gehn', he wrote in his
diary on 21 March 1780, 'Sitzend bin ich zu nichts aufgelegt'. Such move-
ment set the processes of thought in motion and transformed itself into the
rhythmic and metrical movement of poetry, and not just in the energetic
years of his youth. The grand outburst of the Marienbad *Elegie* in 1823 arose
spontaneously in the coach that was carrying Goethe back to Weimar, so
that the poem has, in Goethe's classic understatement, 'eine gewisse Un-
mittelbarkeit' (to Eckermann, 15 November 1823).

Not just the poet but what he sees is in motion and it positively comes to
meet him. In *Maifest* the energies of spring thrust out at him through plant-
growth and bird-song. In *Im Herbst 1775* the vines grow luxuriantly up
towards him. Even the largest things seem to move in response to his
movement: in *Auf dem See* the mountains themselves loom towards him as
the oars lift his boat rhythmically towards them. It is not just a dynamic but
a reciprocating world, it even shares his delight:

> Ich sah die Welt mit liebevollen Blicken
> Und Welt und ich, wir schwelgten im Entzücken.[10]

Thus where many nature poets are fixed contemplators of a static scene,
Goethe is a quantum of natural energy moving and taking pleasure in a
complex of like energies. (That makes the landscape of *Über allen Gipfeln*
all the more striking, a rare moment of complete stillness.) The scenes he sets
are far from being background to an emotional event; they are part of it, a
focus of attention, a participating force, they inspire feeling and help sym-
bolically to transmit it. Even when the poet is in love, he is in love with the
world too, and that gives his conveying of reality a special tone. Realism in
European literature has usually presented bitter truths; it has described and
often protested against social ills, usually through the medium of prose fiction
and drama. Lyrical poems in general are not an obvious vehicle for such
purposes, they are more likely to be responding to the deeper grain beneath
social structures. In Goethe's poems this becomes a positively loving realism.
He states the programme for it in the poem *An Merck*, an informal personal
communication dashed off in 1774, which he never published and probably
forgot. Its message is nonetheless at the heart of Goethe's poetry. The artist,
he says, must love the things of this world, however banal and unprepossess-
ing some of them may be:

Geb Gott dir Lieb zu deinem Pantoffel
Ehr jede krüpliche Kartoffel
Erkenne jedes Dings Gestalt
Sein Leid und Freud Ruh und Gewalt
Und fühle wie die ganze Welt
Der große Himmel zusammenhält.

Once again, the discrete phenomena and the overarching order, evoked in phrases that echo Faust's quest for the deepest secrets of reality – 'Was die Welt Im Innersten zusammenhält'.[11]

Goethe's positive vision does not mean he was turning away from the ills of the social world that overlay the beauty of natural things. He wrote the tragedy of Werther, and of Gretchen in *Faust*, he sketched the harsh plight of the young woman in the poem *Vor Gericht*. He was not blind to the dark side of nature itself, which was all the time implacably destroying as well as endlessly creating. It is nature the consuming monster that dominates Werther's thoughts as he gets closer to his tragic fate.[12] Yet tragedy itself needs a foil, a sense of beauty and value. If there were less to lose, there would be less to lament. Keeping this dual perspective is one mark of a great artist. Strikingly, as radical a writer as Georg Büchner, political activist and author of the most harrowing of German social dramas, *Woyzeck*, shares Goethe's near-ecstatic vision of the world's beauty. In his short story *Lenz*, he sketches a remarkably similar programme through the mouth of the eighteenth-century dramatist whose mental break-up he is narrating. An artist, Lenz declares, must embrace what is living, whether it is beautiful or ugly in the common view; he must enter into the lowliest forms of life and render them in every detail. Lenz gives the example of two country girls he passed by on a walk who had stopped to arrrange their hair. They made a perfect picture, it dissolved in an instant and gave way to a new one:

Die schönsten Bilder, die schwellendsten Töne gruppieren, lösen sich auf. Nur eins bleibt: eine unendliche Schönheit, die aus einer Form in die andre tritt, ewig aufgeblättert, verändert. [...] Man muß die Menschheit lieben, um in das eigentümliche Wesen jedes einzudringen; es darf einem keiner zu gering, keiner zu häßlich sein, erst dann kann man sie verstehen.[13]

That image of reality, Lenz says, is rare in literature; but one place where it is sometimes found, besides Shakespeare and folksong, is in Goethe. Lenz/Büchner's and Goethe's visions do indeed match, right down to that sense of a world of flux and changing forms which yet has an underlying unity and beauty.

4

Goethe's vision is not just a matter of emotional response. It began that way in his youth, and to the end of his life he could react to the world in deeply felt poetry. But over the decades much else enriched and confirmed his perceptions. He led a many-stranded intellectual life, of which the central strand from 1780 on was science – anatomy, geology, botany, meteorology. He was engaged at first hand in observation, experiment, collecting specimens, writing papers. Again like Büchner, who was a professional scientist, Goethe's vision had solider foundations than feeling. His science produced direct poetic results: in his middle years he wrote poems on the morphology of plants and of animals (see the poem *Metamorphose der Tiere*); and in his last decade he published – mostly in scientific journals – a series of poems that combine lyricism with an almost God's-eye-view of the universe to achieve what feels like a mystical revelation.[14] These poems seem to penetrate to the workings of the universe that Faust was so desperate to have revealed to him. Goethe's substitute for Faustian magic has been six decades of devoted wordcraft and four of scientific hard graft.

There was not just science. History, aesthetics, art history, architecture, and a voracious appetite for all the natural and social phenomena a traveller met with, especially during the two years of freedom and study in Italy (1786-8) – all these forms of study together made what German eighteenth-century writers summed up in the term 'anthropology', the study of many-facetted mankind. This comprehensive curiosity and the answers it found are the backing for Goethe's definition of style as something that 'rests on the deepest foundations of knowledge, on the essential nature of things, insofar as we are allowed access to it in visible and graspable shapes'.[15] Like his model of communication, this is almost defiantly optimistic, with only a small concession ('insofar...') to the epistemological doubters and problematisers. Add to the life of study and science his ministerial involvement in running the mini-state of Sachsen-Weimar – a more practical and hands-on involvement precisely because the Duchy was so small – and it is clear Goethe was linked into reality more closely and in more varied ways than most people, and certainly most writers, then or now.

That is not gainsaid by the fact that he spent his whole life from the age of twenty-six in one place, the small and politically insignificant provincial town of Weimar. As with that equally unbudging fixture Immanuel Kant in far-flung Königsberg, Goethe's range was European. Europe increasingly came to him, Napoleon included. Meantime Goethe was always mentally on the move, across Europe and beyond Europe, enriching his poetic repertoire from cultures distant in space and time: ancient Greece and Rome, medieval Persia, China. The core personality remains recognisable through the guise of their varying conventions. And besides all conventions, there was still, as in the final Dornburg poems, the possibility of the simple personal voice, the individual speaking 'aus sich heraus.' That, the historic turn for which Goethe was in large measure responsible, is sometimes said to be itself a convention. If so, it is one so wide and liberating that we have yet to reach its limits.

Notes to the Introduction

1. *Dichtung und Wahrheit*, Book 7. HA 9, 283.

2. To Johann Caspar Lavater and Johann Conrad Pfenninger, 26 April 1774. HA Br 1, 159.

3. See Wulf Segebrecht, *Das Gelegenheitsgedicht. Ein Beitrag zur Geschichte und Poetik der deutschen Lyrik*, Stuttgart 1977.

4. See 'An Gott', in *Ausgewählte Werke*, ed. Karl August Schleiden, Munich 1962, p. 47.

5. *Die Briefe der Frau Rat Goethe*, ed. Albert Köster, 2 vols., Leipzig 1911.

6. Immanuel Kant, *Beantwortung der Frage: Was ist Aufklärung?* 1784.

7. Georg Simmel, *Kant*, Leipzig 1904, p. 180.

8. *Noch ein Wort für junge Dichter*, HA 12, 360.

9. '...daß irgendeiner das Speziale so ins Allgemeine emporgehoben, daß sie es wieder in ihre eigene Spezialität übernehmen können.' To Carl Friedrich Zelter, 27 March 1830. HA Br 4, 375.

10. *Zu meinen Handzeichnungen*, I (1821).

11. *Faust Erster Teil*, 'Nacht', lines 382f.

12. *Die Leiden des jungen Werther*, Erstes Buch, 18. August, HA 6, 53.

13. Georg Büchner, *Lenz* (1836). In his lecture *Über Schädelnerven* of the following year, Büchner similarly speaks – in his own voice, and as a scientist – of an ultimate 'Gesetz der Schönheit' that underlies all natural phenomena.

14. Cf. the letter of 1 September 1816 to Wilhelm von Humboldt: 'daß man selber zum Seher, das heißt: Gott ähnlich wird [...] ist doch am Ende der Triumph aller Poesie'.

15. '...so ruht der Stil auf den tiefsten Grundfesten der Erkenntnis, auf dem Wesen der Dinge, insofern uns erlaubt ist, es in sichtbaren und greiflichen Gestalten zu erkennen.' *Über einfache Nachahmung der Natur, Manier, Stil* (1789) HA 12, 32.

BIBLIOGRAPHY

The text

The text of Goethe's poems in this volume is based on the standard modern editions, as listed below, preserving original spellings and other linguistic forms in the earlier texts. Preference has largely been given to early rather than revised versions, which is as much a critical as an editorial decision. It rests on a view of Goethe's strengths as a uniquely spontaneous poet, and the tendency of his first thoughts to be measurably better than his deliberate later adjustments. An edition of this kind has not the space to argue out every case in detail, but the essential issues should be clear from representative instances discussed in the commentary – for example, the changes to *Mir schlug das Herz*, the variants of *An Schwager Kronos*, and the missing line in *Das Göttliche*. In two cases, the versions of a poem are printed on facing pages to allow full and direct comparison.

With few exceptions (the second *Wandrers Nachtlied* and the revised versions of two early pieces) the poems are arranged in chronological order, to reflect the fact that a lyrical corpus as much as the individual poem has an organic development, if on a larger scale. That in itself makes it indispensable to print the poem recording a given moment in the version which that moment engendered. Criticism has surprisingly often used, for example, versions revised in the late eighties as documents of what the young Goethe was feeling and achieving. Something of a breakthrough came with Trunz's edition of the poems in the Hamburger Ausgabe (see below), which, though still questionable on certain details, did at least put early versions where they belonged, and in crucial instances printed early and late side by side. All of which leads on to:

Editions

Goethes Werke, Hamburger Ausgabe, ed. Erich Trunz (Hamburg 1948 and reprints; revised edition 1981 and reprints [= **HA**]). This edition marked the return of sane scholarship after the cultural darkness of the Nazi years. The general editor Trunz himself edited vol. 1, a selection of the poems, and vol. 2, the *West-östlicher Divan*. The extensive commentary, especially in vol. 1, amounts to a full interpretation both of individual poems (for which Trunz draws on and quotes from many other critics) and of Goethe's poetic and intellectual development overall. Now half a century old, the edition has worn well and still provides a persuasive framework.

Goethes Gedichte, ed. Emil Staiger (Zurich 1949). The commentary to this three-volume edition, virtually complete except for the *West-östlicher Divan*, limits itself largely to explaining details of word, syntax and allusion, and refrains from interpretation. It is thus helpful to the student in a way different from and complementary to Trunz.

Gedichte 1756-1799, and *Gedichte 1800-1832*, ed. Karl Eibl (Frankfurt am Main 1987 and 1988 [= **Eibl 1** and **Eibl 2**]). The first two volumes of the edition Goethe: *Sämtliche Werke*, Deutscher Klassiker Verlag. Editorially meticulous, barring the occasional misprint, and now the widely preferred text. Eibl proceeds chronologically, printing Goethe's own successive collections, which makes clear the processes of change both within the single poem and in Goethe's overall conception of his lyrical oeuvre. The commentary is workmanlike and informative, without interpretative pretensions.

Goethe: *Sämtliche Werke*, ed. Karl Richter (Munich 1985ff. [=**MA**]). This edition presents Goethe's whole oeuvre chronologically, so that works of whatever literary genre or none (e.g. administrative and scientific writings) appear cheek by jowl in the same volume, purely as their date of composition dictates. This gives a wonderful sense of Goethe's many sidedness, and can fruitfully bring out connections that normally pass unnoticed; but it also means that poems and their accompanying commentaries are scattered through all the volumes of the edition.

Goethe: *West-östlicher Divan*, ed. Max Rychner (Zurich 1963). A companion volume to the Staiger edition listed above, with an excellent commentary.

Goethe: *Erotische Gedichte*, ed. Andreas Ammer (Frankfurt am Main 1991[insel taschenbuch 1225]). Includes material not found elsewhere, and attempts to reconstruct the original version of the *Römische Elegien*.

Goethe: *Erotic Poems*, ed. David Luke and Hans Rudolf Vaget (Oxford 1997). A bilingual edition, with verse translations by Luke, of the *Römische Elegien*, the *Venezianische Epigramme*, and the erotic morality-tale *Das Tagebuch*.

Goethe: *Elegie von Marienbad*, ed. Jürgen Behrens and Christoph Michel (Frankfurt am Main 1991 [insel taschenbuch 1250]). Documents the genesis of the *Elegie*.

Letters are quoted mainly from the 4-volume selection uniform with the Hamburger Ausgabe, ed. Karl Robert Mandelkow, Hamburg 1962-7 [=**HABr**].

Biographies

George Henry Lewes, *Life and Works of Goethe* (1855). The very first biography in any language and still, for all its Victorian flavour, highly readable.

Nicholas Boyle, *Goethe. The Poet and the Age*. A monumental undertaking, of which only the first volume has yet appeared (*The Poetry of Desire. 1749-1790* [Oxford 1991]). Already covers a significant part of Goethe's poetic career, and is essential reading while waiting for further instalments.

John R. Williams, *The Life of Goethe* (Oxford 1998). A complete, more compact account of the life, with good discussions of individual works.

T.J.Reed, *Goethe*, (Oxford Past Masters: Oxford, 1984; second edition 1998). A concise introduction to Goethe's life and all aspects of his work.

Critical work on the poetry

The most comprehensive and detailed treatment is now volume 1 of the new *Goethe-Handbuch*, ed. Regine Otto and Bernd Witte (Stuttgart 1996 [=**GHb**]). It contains general articles on the phases of Goethe's creative life and interpretations of individual poems, each with its own bibliography. (Volumes 2 and 3 are devoted to Goethe's dramas and prose writings respectively; volume 4 is an encyclopedic reference work.)

The special Goethe number of the journal *German Life and Letters*, vol. xxxvi, double issue 1/2 (1983 [=**GLL**]) contains valuable essays on the following poems of the present edition: *Willkommen und Abschied*; *Maifest*; *Auf dem See*; *Wandrers Nachtlied* 2; *Warum gabst du uns die tiefen Blicke*; *Römische Elegien* V and VII; *Urworte. Orphisch*; and *Trilogie der Leidenschaft*.

The best single book on Goethe's poetry remains Max Kommerell's *Gedanken über Gedichte* (Frankfurt am Main 1943): sensitive criticism remarkably untouched by the pressures of its period. Kommerell's aperçus and thumbnail sketches of individual poems, and his broader comments on particular poetic forms and phases, are the work of a fine intuitive critic.

Goethe, *Alle Freuden, die unendlichen*, ed. Marcel Reich-Ranicki (Frankfurt am Main 1987 [Insel-Bücherei 1028]) is a collection of essays on Goethe's love poems, including (of the poems in our volume) *Willkommen und Abschied, Mailied, Heidenröslein, Ganymed, Vor Gericht, Erlkönig, Kennst du das Land, Römische Elegien* V. These short interpretations are ideal first pieces for students learning to approach German criticism.

Klaus Weimar, *Goethes Gedichte 1769-1775. Interpretationen zu einem Anfang* (Paderborn 1982) offers a coherent reading of Goethe's early poetry, judiciously carrying forward the findings of each interpretation to illuminate the ones that follow. The individual interpretations, products of a Zurich seminar, argue closely and concretely. The volume would be a good next step in following critical argument in German.

David Wellbery, *The Specular Moment. Goethe's Early Lyric and the Beginnings of Romanticism* (Stanford University Press 1996) is the most ambitious recent book on the poetry. It declares its method as 'discourse analysis', i.e. a study of the poems' linguistic system that purports to refrain from actually interpreting them. The book's own system makes no concessions to easy readability; but whether or not one agrees with Wellbery's premisses and procedures, they generate much acute observation of fine detail from which the student can profit.

For the rest, the literature on individual poems is endless. A short selection would be arbitrary, a long one oppressive. Since the works listed above, all except the sovereignly self-sufficient Kommerell, have their own bibliographies, the user of this edition is encouraged to work outwards from its text and commentary to whichever of them is readily available. From the discussion there of any particular poem, the trail can then be followed further through the focused mini-bibliographies they provide – always remembering that poetry, Goethe's more than anyone's, speaks direct to readers, and that the secondary literature designed to shed light on problems must not be allowed to block out the light that comes from the poem itself.

A NOTE ON METRE

(or how to read a Goethe poem)

German is a language with strong natural stresses and corresponding un-stressed elements, which together create a clearly audible variety. The units (or 'feet') of poetic metre are the possible combinations of stressed (/) and unstressed (x) syllables that occur naturally in the language. The commonest are:

iamb	x /	Gesang
trochee	/ x	ewig
dactyl	/ x x	herrliche
anapaest	x x /	unterbricht

Since these sequences are there in the language before it ever gets as far as poetry, they are not hard to recognise and grasp when it does. That should give the confidence to read poems aloud, if only to oneself, which is an enjoy-able and also a necessary part of the experience of poetry, for nothing so brings out a poem's overall direction and meaning or so sharpens its emotional impact.

Whether reading aloud or hearing the poem in the mind's ear, the basic principle is to stick to the way words are normally pronounced, and the metre will largely look after itself. Where the two are at odds, the stresses and rhythm of speech take priority. This allows the variations to be heard which are always present within an outwardly regular metre. They occur in the first place because, at the level of micro-measurement, even similar-seeming words rarely have *exactly* identical rhythm, stress and duration. Vowels vary in length – even the long vowels vary minutely among themselves – and a word with a consonant cluster in it will take slightly longer to speak. Try comparing, say, 'Freudetaumel' with 'Einschiffmorgen' ('-ffm-'!) from the poem *Seefahrt*, or 'gar nicht da' and 'noch so fern' from *Dem aufgehenden Vollmonde*. There are also subtly different degrees of stress, and some analysts of metre register a minor (\ ) as well as a major (/) stress. Beyond giving one example below, I leave this on one side for the sake of simplicity.

But then beyond the variations inherent in the patterns of the spoken language, there are more important variations that are part of the poem's expressive effect. For example, the middle section of the poem *Auf dem See* has a *trochaic* rhythm: '**Aug**, mein **Aug**, was sinkst du nieder' (/ x). Yet the last line of that section (line 12) opens with two stressed syllables together:

'hier auch' (/ /) a so-called *spondee*, rarely found in German. The double emphasis underpins what the words are saying, namely that what this present moment offers is equal to what the speaker remembers in his seductive dreams of the past. So while rhythmic regularity can build up the power of an utterance, as in the second stanza of *Willkommen und Abschied*, a rhythm that runs counter to the pattern can mark a necessary contrast, or (as here) a turning point.

Again, in the poem *Kennst du das Land, wo die Zitronen blühn?* the metre is overall *iambic* (x /). But the poem's opening words, which are also the opening words of the other stanzas, reverse that sequence and are *trochaic* (/ x): 'Kennst du...?' It is perfectly natural speech. Yet to open with that stressed syllable against the run of what becomes the settled rhythm strengthens the feeling of an immediate unprepared appeal. The rest of the line is no more regular, and reads naturally as:

Kennst du das Land, wo die Zitronen blühn?

Overall, then, instead of: x / x / x / x / x /
                  we have: / x x / x x x / x \
(The last syllable, 'blühn', would be a case of minor or secondary stress.)

This is not to claim subtle significance for absolutely every shift in the rhythm away from the regular metre. The point rather is that in poetry, especially the poetry of highly personal expression that Goethe helped to establish, there are usually two rhythms at work whose counterpoint is part of the pleasure. We hear the natural spoken rhythm moving and changing within the fixed rhythm or metre. If the poet keeps too rigidly to the set rhythm, the result may feel coldly formal, dead. If he departs from it too freely and frequently, the beneficial pressure of a set form may be lost. Somewhere between these extremes, speech rhythm and metrical rhythm make a complex and satisfying counterpoint. We hear, in Wordsworth's phrase, 'a man speaking to men', but we hear it concentrated and heightened by the constraints of form. It is natural speech *plus*. And perhaps the counterpoint characteristic of an individual is what we are recognising when we hear an unfamiliar poem with a familiar sound and say 'That must be by...'. Perhaps it is what Nietzsche meant when he said, 'Jeder Geist hat seinen Klang'.

The principle of following the normal rhythms of speech will help the reader through the thickets, as they may seem at first, of Goethe's *Classical metres*. Not that he uses many. Unlike Hölderlin, who took over all the major lyrical stanzas of the ancients, Goethe sticks to the two commonest and simplest forms, the *hexameter*, a six-foot line that can be used by itself, as in his scientific poem *Metamorphose der Tiere* or his mini-epic *Hermann und*

Dorothea (the two traditional uses for the hexameter in Latin); and the *pentameter*, which can only occur along with the hexameter, as the second element in a pair known as a *distich* or *elegiac couplet*. Again traditionally, Goethe uses this form in the love poems of the *Römische Elegien*.

Far from being any kind of alien form imposed on the German language, these metres actually helped free its inherent rhythms. Crucially, both hexameter and pentameter take their shape above all from the *dactyl*, and this foot can accommodate a whole range of German words and expressions that the shorter feet, iamb or trochee, cannot. Nor can they in English, of course. We are so used to the iambic movement of Shakespeare's blank verse that we fail to realise how many natural phrases and cadences it excludes – or would exclude, if Shakespeare allowed it to by keeping rigidly to the metrical pattern. Which he does not. For example he has dactyls in both the first two lines in Hamlet's 'To be or not to be' soliloquy: 'That is the question', and 'Whether 'tis nobler...'. Similarly in German, a phrase like 'Laß dich, Geliebte, nicht reun' – and such combinations are legion in the language – will not fit into the rigid alternation of one stressed, one unstressed syllable, whichever way round you arrange them, as iamb or trochee; but it makes a perfect dactyl. So Goethe's turn to the verse-forms of the Classical languages paradoxically brought his poetry even closer to the idiomatic naturalness that was already its strength.

It is hardly necessary to know the background in Antiquity to all this – for example that the Latin original metres worked primarily with *quantity*, that is to say, how long the vowels in words were. Thus the *dactyl* foot was 'long – short – short', the spondee 'long – long'. There was almost certainly also some kind of rhythm counterpointing this schema, but its secret has been lost. Except when put off his stroke by would-be Classical authorities of the day who misguidedly pressed him to apply the Latin principle of quantity (his few adjustments are decidedly 'Verschlimmbesserungen') Goethe simply translated the sequence of long – short into a sequence of stressed – unstressed. So did most of the other German poets who adapted Classical metres. The dactyl thus became / x x. The spondee (/ /) was replaced altogether by a trochee (/ x), since the two consecutive stresses of the spondee, as mentioned above apropos *Auf dem See*, occur too rarely in German to make part of a usable scheme.

The hexameter and pentameter are made even more flexible by the licence to mix the feet in whatever proportion and sequence suits the poem's purposes. In the *hexameter*, the first four feet can be any mixture of dactyl and trochee – all the one, all the other, or any selection. There is an obvious difference between a line with nothing but trochees (ponderous, slow) and one composed of all dactyls (almost waltzing). The various combinations between these extremes can fine-tune the rhythmic effect. The only constraint on the poet is that the last two feet have to be dactyl-plus-trochee in that order, giving the line its characteristic bouncing close: / x x / x. Somewhere in the middle of the line will be a natural resting or pivoting point, a 'cut' or *caesura*. That too will be determined by natural speech rhythms and sense groupings.

The *pentameter*, despite its name, is not straightforwardly a five-foot line, like the iambic pentameter that dominates English verse. Goethe's pentameter has two sections of two-and-a-half feet each, which add up to five. The halves are separated by a very marked central caesura; and a very audible pause at the end of the line gives it a highly symmetrical effect. Since both the caesura and the end-pause follow a heavily stressed syllable, the pentameter is in a sense a hexameter with silences replacing the unstressed syllables of its third and its sixth foot. The first two feet can be either dactyl or trochee; the third and fourth full feet must both be dactyls.

Examples: ([C] = caesura)

Hexameter

```
  1        2      3          4      5              6
/ x x   /  x  x/ x  x   / x   /     x   x /  x
Hero erblickte Leandern am lauten Fest [C] und behende
```

Pentameter

```
  1           2   ¹/₂        3         4      ¹/₂
/   x  x   / x  x  /      /  x  x   / x  x   /
Stürzte der Liebende sich [C] heiß in die nächtliche Flut.
```

None of this needs to be a problem, or even to be acquired as discursive 'knowledge' by a reader who simply wants to know how the verse should sound when read aloud or heard in the mind's ear. To restate the guiding principle: follow normal pronunciation and stress patterns, and the metre will look after itself. It helps to know that both hexameter and pentameter have an initial stress. Just occasionally one may have to start a line over again, since there are options on whether or not to stress some words. In the first line of *Römische Elegien* III, 'daß du mir so schnell dich ergeben', 'du' is stressed but 'dich' is not. According to circumstance and meaning, these personal pronouns and other monosyllables – particles, adverbs, or conjunctions, such as 'doch', 'nun' or 'daß' – can be dwelt on or touched on more lightly. This is part of the hexameter's and pentameter's user-friendliness to the poet, and makes no undue problems for readers.

It should be clear from this sketch that metre is a flexible thing, and that Goethe treats it with a freedom that comes from instinctively giving priority to the natural run of language, not to convention. This leads on to the final important verse-form – or rather, form of verse – that Goethe used, in which language operates without any fixed pattern at all and is moulded by the needs of the occasion. In his youth only, but at that time with immense force and effect, he wrote what is commonly called free verse. Part of his inspiration came from the Greek poet Pindar, whose complex stanza forms were thought to be free verse by eighteenth-century readers. Thus, long before Goethe's Classical period, he was already drawing on ancient sources.

T.S. Eliot shrewdly remarked that there was no such thing as free verse, only good verse, bad verse, and chaos. That is to say, if verse is good it cannot be free, even though it may not be metrically regular. Word-groupings, rhythms, line-breaks – everything must be shaped by the necessities of the poem, must grow out of the physical realities, feelings, inner movements it embodies. Thus the rhythms of *An Schwager Kronos* match the brisk departure, 'Fort den rasselnden Trott', then the dragging uphill movement as the coach goes 'mühsam Berg hinauf', till the view at the top opens out in the leisurely spread of stressed syllables, 'weit hoch herrlich der Blick'. Prometheus' defiance of Zeus is plainly audible in the stolid 'Mußt mir meine Erde Doch lassen stehn'. Here it would be possible to stress everything but the final 'e' in 'meine', 'Erde' and 'lassen'. Short of that, there is a decisive final stress which is made possible by exchanging the normal word-order with its falling rhythm ('stehen lassen') for one with archaic echoes of Luther; while the abrupt 'Ich dich ehren? Wofür?' is a dismissive vocal gesture that gives force to what the words say. In a different key again, the first stanza of *Ganymed* conveys the dense sequence of perceptions pressing in on the speaker. Later the clouds' movement downward to lift him from the earth is imitated by the line-breaks – '...die Wolken // Abwärts, die Wolken // Neigen sich' – and his aspiration upwards is felt in the rhythms of 'Hinauf, hinauf strebt's' and 'Mir! mir'. Examples could be multiplied, but these few may suggest the range of effects free verse gives the reader to explore and reflect on. More than regular verse, it invites and rewards the extra bit of empathy that can recognise the aptness of a sound-shape the poet has created from nothing – or rather from his own rhythmic resources and the pulse within the words.

Such creation is the other half of a dual principle: that all good regular verse is gently freeing itself from pattern and all good free verse is subtly creating it. That, from different directions, confirms that at the heart of modern poetry is the distinctive individual sensibility with its unique voice.

An den Schlaf

Der du mit deinem Mohne
Selbst Götteraugen zwingst,
Und Bettler oft zum Throne
Zum Mädgen Schäfer bringst,
Vernimm; Kein Traumgespinste   5
Verlang' ich heut' von dir,
Den größten deiner Dienste
Geliebter, leiste mir.

An meines Mädgens Seite
Sitz' ich, ihr Aug' spricht Lust,   10
Und unter neid'scher Seide
Steigt fühlbar ihre Brust,
Oft hatte meinen Küssen
Sie Amor zugebracht,
Dies Glück muß ich vermissen   15
Die strenge Mutter wacht.

Am Abend triffst du wieder
Mich dort, O tritt herein,
Sprüh' Mohn von dem Gefieder,
Da schlaf die Mutter ein: 20
Bei blassem Lichterscheinen
Von Lieb' Annette warm,
Sink', wie Mama in deinen,
In meinen gier'gen Arm.

Die Nacht

Gern verlaß ich diese Hütte,
Meiner Liebsten Aufenthalt,
Wandle mit verhülltem Tritte
Durch den ausgestorbnen Wald.
Luna bricht die Nacht der Eichen,   5
Zephirs melden ihren Lauf,
Und die Birken streun mit Neigen
Ihr den süßen Weihrauch auf.

1

Schauer, der das Herze fühlen,
Der die Seele schmelzen macht,   10
Flüstert durchs Gebüsch im Kühlen.
Welche schöne, süße Nacht!
Freude! Wollust! Kaum zu fassen!
Und doch wollt' ich, Himmel, dir
Tausend solcher Nächte lassen,   15
Gäb' mein Mädgen Eine mir.

An Behrisch, 3. Ode

Sei gefühllos!
Ein leichtbewegtes Herz,
Ist ein elend Gut
Auf der wankenden Erde.

Behrisch, des Frühlings Lächeln   5
Erheitre Deine Stirne nie,
Nie trübt sie dann mit Verdruß
Des Winters stürmischer Ernst.

Lehne Dich nie an des Mädgens
Sorgenverwiegende Brust,   10
Nie auf des Freundes
Elendtragenden Arm.

Schon versammelt
Von seiner Klippenwarte
Der Neid, auf Dich   15
Den ganzen, luchsgleichen Blick.

Dehnt die Klauen
Stürzt und schlägt
Hinterlistig sie
Dir in die Schultern.   20

Stark sind die magern Arme,
Wie Panther Arme,
Er schüttelt Dich
Und reißt Dich los.

Tod ist Trennung, 25
Dreifacher Tod
Trennung ohne Hoffnung
Wiederzusehn.

Gerne verließest Du
Dieses gehaßte Land, 30
Hielte Dich nicht Freundschaft
Mit Blumenfesseln an mir.

Zerreiß sie! Ich klage nicht.
Kein edler Freund
Hält den Mitgefangnen 35
Der fliehn kann zurück.

Der Gedanke
Von des Freundes Freiheit,
Ist ihm Freiheit
Im Kerker. 40

Du gehst, ich bleibe.
Aber schon drehen
Des letzten Jahrs Flügelspeichen
Sich um die rauchende Achse.

Ich zähle die Schläge 45
Des donnernden Rads,
Segne den letzten,
Da springen die Riegel, frei bin ich wie Du.

Heidenröslein

Sah ein Knab' ein Röslein stehn,
Röslein auf der Heiden,
War so jung und morgenschön,
Lief er schnell es nah zu sehn,
Sah's mit vielen Freuden. 5
Röslein, Röslein, Röslein rot,
Röslein auf der Heiden.

Knabe sprach: ich breche dich,
Röslein auf der Heiden!
Röslein sprach: ich steche dich, 10
Daß du ewig denkst an mich,
Und ich will's nicht leiden.
Röslein, Röslein, Röslein rot,
Röslein auf der Heiden.

Und der wilde Knabe brach 15
's Röslein auf der Heiden;
Röslein wehrte sich und stach,
Half ihr doch kein Weh und Ach,
Mußt es eben leiden.
Röslein, Röslein, Röslein rot, 20
Röslein auf der Heiden.

Maifest

Wie herrlich leuchtet
Mir die Natur!
Wie glänzt die Sonne!
Wie lacht die Flur!

Es dringen Blüten 5
Aus jedem Zweig,
Und tausend Stimmen
Aus dem Gesträuch,

Und Freud und Wonne
Aus jeder Brust. 10
O Erd O Sonne
O Glück O Lust!

O Lieb' O Liebe,
So golden schön,
Wie Morgenwolken 15
Auf jenen Höhn;

Du segnest herrlich
Das frische Feld,

Im Blütendampfe
Die volle Welt.   20

O Mädchen Mädchen,
Wie lieb' ich dich!
Wie blinkt dein Auge!
Wie liebst du mich!

So liebt die Lerche   25
Gesang und Luft,
Und Morgenblumen
Den Himmels Duft,

Wie ich dich liebe
Mit warmen Blut,   30
Die du mir Jugend
Und Freud und Mut

Zu neuen Liedern,
Und Tänzen gibst!
Sei ewig glücklich   35
Wie du mich liebst!

Mir schlug das Herz

Mir schlug das Herz; geschwind zu Pferde,
Und fort, wild, wie ein Held zur Schlacht!
Der Abend wiegte schon die Erde,
Und an den Bergen hing die Nacht;
Schon stund im Nebelkleid die Eiche,   5
Ein aufgetürmter Riese, da,
Wo Finsternis aus dem Gesträuche
Mit hundert schwarzen Augen sah.

Der Mond von seinem Wolkenhügel,
Schien kläglich aus dem Duft hervor;   10
Die Winde schwangen leise Flügel,
Umsausten schauerlich mein Ohr;
Die Nacht schuf tausend Ungeheuer—
Doch tausendfacher war mein Mut;
Mein Geist war ein verzehrend Feuer,   15
Mein ganzes Herz zerfloß in Glut.

Ich sah dich, und die milde Freude
Floß aus dem süßen Blick auf mich.
Ganz war mein Herz an deiner Seite,
Und jeder Atemzug für dich.   20
Ein rosenfarbes Frühlings Wetter
Lag auf dem lieblichen Gesicht,
Und Zärtlichkeit für mich, ihr Götter!
Ich hofft' es, ich verdient' es nicht.

Der Abschied, wie bedrängt, wie trübe!   25
Aus deinen Blicken sprach dein Herz.
In deinen Küssen, welche Liebe,
O welche Wonne, welcher Schmerz!
Du gingst, ich stund, und sah zur Erden,
Und sah dir nach mit nassem Blick;   30
Und doch, welch Glück! geliebt zu werden,
Und lieben, Götter, welch ein Glück.

Willkommen und Abschied

Es schlug mein Herz, geschwind zu Pferde!
Es war getan fast eh' gedacht;
Der Abend wiegte schon die Erde,
Und an den Bergen hing die Nacht:
Schon stand im Nebelkleid die Eiche,   5
Ein aufgetürmter Riese, da,
Wo Finsternis aus dem Gesträuche
Mit hundert schwarzen Augen sah.

Der Mond von einem Wolkenhügel
Sah kläglich aus dem Duft hervor,   10
Die Winde schwangen leise Flügel,
Umsaus'ten schauerlich mein Ohr;
Die Nacht schuf tausend Ungeheuer;
Doch frisch und fröhlich war mein Mut:
In meinen Adern welches Feuer!   15
In meinem Herzen welche Glut!

Dich sah ich, und die milde Freude
Floß von dem süßen Blick auf mich,
Ganz war mein Herz an deiner Seite,
Und jeder Atemzug für dich.   20
Ein rosenfarbnes Frühlingswetter
Umgab das liebliche Gesicht,
Und Zärtlichkeit für mich — Ihr Götter!
Ich hofft' es, ich verdient' es nicht!

Doch ach! schon mit der Morgensonne   25
Verengt der Abschied mir das Herz:
In deinen Küssen, welche Wonne!
In deinem Auge, welcher Schmerz!
Ich ging, du standst und sahst zur Erden,
Und sahst mir nach mit nassem Blick: 30
Und doch, welch Glück geliebt zu werden!
Und lieben, Götter, welch ein Glück!

Gretchen am Spinnrade

Meine Ruh ist hin,
Mein Herz ist schwer;
Ich finde sie nimmer
Und nimmermehr.

Wo ich ihn nicht hab,   5
Ist mir das Grab,
Die ganze Welt
Ist mir vergällt.

Mein armer Kopf
Ist mir verrückt,   10
Mein armer Sinn
Ist mir zerstückt.

Meine Ruh ist hin,
Mein Herz ist schwer;
Ich finde sie nimmer   15
Und nimmermehr.

Nach ihm nur schau ich
Zum Fenster hinaus,
Nach ihm nur geh ich
Aus dem Haus.   20

Sein hoher Gang,
Sein' edle Gestalt,
Seines Mundes Lächeln,
Seiner Augen Gewalt

Und seiner Rede   25
Zauberfluß,
Sein Händedruck
Und, ach, sein Kuß!

Meine Ruh ist hin,
Mein Herz ist schwer;   30
Ich finde sie nimmer
Und nimmermehr.

Mein Schoß, Gott! drängt
Sich nach ihm hin.
Ach dürft ich fassen   35
Und halten ihn

Und küssen ihn
So wie ich wollt,
An seinen Küssen
Vergehen sollt!   40

Wandrers Sturmlied

Wen du nicht verlässest Genius   1
Nicht der Regen nicht der Sturm
Haucht ihm Schauer übers Herz
Wen du nicht verlässest Genius,
Wird der Regen Wolk   5
Wird dem Schlossensturm
Entgegensingen wie die
Lerche du dadroben

Den du nicht verlässest Genius
Wirst ihn heben übern Schlammpfad   10
Mit den Feuerflügeln
Wandeln wird er
Wie mit Blumenfüßen
Über Deukalions Flutschlamm
Python tötend leicht groß   15
Pythius Apollo
Den du nicht verlässest Genius

Dem du nicht verlässest Genius
Wirst die wollnen Flügel unterspreiten
Wenn er auf dem Felsen schläft   20
Wirst mit Hüterfittigen ihn decken
In des Haines Mitternacht.

Wen du nicht verlässest Genius
Wirst im Schneegestöber Wärm umhüllen
Nach der Wärme ziehn sich Musen   25

Nach der Wärme Charitinnen,
Wen du nicht verlässest Genius.

Umschwebt mich ihr Musen!
Ihr Charitinnen!
Das ist Wasser das ist Erde   30
Und der Sohn des Wassers und der Erde
Über den ich wandle Göttergleich

Ihr seid rein wie das Herz der Wasser
Ihr seid rein wie das Mark der Erde
Ihr umschwebt mich und ich schwebe   35
Über Wasser über Erde
Göttergleich.

Soll der zurückkehren
Der kleine schwarze feurige Bauer
Soll der zurückkehren, erwartend   40
Nur deine Gaben Vater Bromius
Und helleuchtend umwärmend Feuer
Soll der zurückkehren mutig,
Und ich den ihr begleitet
Musen und Charitinnen all   45
Den Alls erwartet was ihr
Musen und Charitinnen
Umkränzende Seeligkeit
Rings ums Leben verherrlicht habt,
Soll mutlos kehren?   50

Vater Bromius
Du bist Genius
Jahrhunderts Genius
Bist was innre Glut
Pindarn war   55
Was der Welt
Phöb Apoll ist.

Weh weh innre Wärme
Seelen Wärme
Mittelpunkt   60
Glüh ihm entgegen

Phöb Apollen
Kalt wird sonst
Sein Fürstenblick
Über dich vorüber gleiten   65
Neidgetroffen
Auf der Ceder Grün verweilen
Die zu grünen
Sein nicht harrt

Warum nennt mein Lied dich zuletzt?   70
Dich von dem es begann
Dich in dem es endet
Dich aus dem es quoll
Jupiter Pluvius.
Dich dich strömt mein Lied   75
Jupiter Pluvius.
Und Castalischer Quell
Quillt ein Nebenbach,
Quillet müßigen
Sterblich Glücklichen   80
Abseits von dir
Jupiter Pluvius
Der du mich fassend deckst
Jupiter Pluvius

Nicht am Ulmen Baum   85
Hast du ihn besucht
Mit dem Tauben Paar
In dem zärtlichen Arm
Mit der freundlichen Ros umkränzt
Tändelnden ihn blumenglücklichen   90
Anakreon,
Sturmatmende Gottheit.
Nicht im Pappelwald
An des Sibaris Strand
In dem hohen Gebürg nicht   95
Dessen Stirn die
Allmächtige Sonne beglänzt
Faßtest du ihn
Den Bienen singenden
Honig lallenden   100

Freundlich winkenden
Theokrit.

Wenn die Räder rasselten Rad an Rad
Rasch ums Ziel weg
Hoch flog siegdurchglühter Jünglinge Peitschenknall   105
Und sich Staub wälzt
Wie von Gebürg herab sich
Kieselwetter ins Tal wälzt
Glühte deine Seel Gefahren Pindar
Mut Pindar — Glühte —   110
Armes Herz —
Dort auf dem Hügel —
Himmlische Macht —
Nur so viel Glut —
Dort ist meine Hütte —   115
Zu waten bis dort hin.

Prometheus

Bedecke deinen Himmel Zeus
Mit Wolkendunst!
Und übe Knabengleich
Der Disteln köpft
An Eichen dich und Bergeshöhn!   5
Mußt mir meine Erde
Doch lassen stehn,
Und meine Hütte
Die du nicht gebaut,
Und meinen Herd   10
Um dessen Glut
Du mich beneidest.

Ich kenne nichts ärmers
Unter der Sonn als euch Götter.
Ihr nähret kümmerlich   15
Von Opfersteuern
Und Gebetshauch
Eure Majestät
Und darbtet wären

12

Nicht Kinder und Bettler   20
Hoffnungsvolle Toren.

Da ich ein Kind war
Nicht wußt wo aus wo ein
Kehrt mein verirrtes Aug
Zur Sonne als wenn drüber wär   25
Ein Ohr zu hören meine Klage
Ein Herz wie meins
Sich des Bedrängten zu erbarmen.

Wer half mir wider
Der Titanen Übermut   30
Wer rettete vom Tode mich
Von Sklaverei?
Hast du's nicht alles selbst vollendet
Heilig glühend Herz?
Und glühtest jung und gut,   35
Betrogen, Rettungsdank
Dem Schlafenden dadroben

Ich dich ehren? Wofür?
Hast du die Schmerzen gelindert
Je des Beladenen   40
Hast du die Tränen gestillet
Je des Geängsteten?
Hat nicht mich zum Manne geschmiedet
Die allmächtige Zeit
Und das ewige Schicksal   45
Meine Herrn und deine?

Wähntest etwa
Ich sollt das Leben hassen
In Wüsten fliehen,
Weil nicht alle Knabenmorgen   50
Blütenträume reiften

Hier sitz ich, forme Menschen
Nach meinem Bilde
Ein Geschlecht das mir gleich sei
Zu leiden, weinen   55

Genießen und zu freuen sich
Und dein nicht zu achten
Wie ich!

Ganymed

Wie im Morgenrot
Du rings mich anglühst
Frühling Geliebter!
Mit tausendfacher Liebeswonne
Sich an mein Herz drängt   5
Deiner ewigen Wärme
Heilig Gefühl
Unendliche Schöne!

Daß ich dich fassen möcht
In diesen Arm!   10

Ach an deinem Busen
Lieg ich, schmachte,
Und deine Blumen dein Gras
Drängen sich an mein Herz
Du kühlst den brennenden   15
Durst meines Busens
Lieblicher Morgenwind!
Ruft drein die Nachtigall
Liebend nach mir aus dem Nebeltal.

Ich komme! Ich komme!   20
Wohin? Ach wohin?

Hinauf hinauf strebts!
Es schweben die Wolken
Abwärts die Wolken
Neigen sich der sehnenden Liebe.   25
Mir! Mir
In eurem Schoße
Aufwärts!
Umfangend umfangen!
Aufwärts   30
An deinem Busen
Alliebender Vater!

An Merck

Hier schick ich dir ein teures Pfand
Das ich mit eigner hoher Hand
Mit Zirkel rein und Lineal
Gefertigt dir zur Zeichen Schal.
Und auch zu festem Kraft und Grund
In einer guten Zeichen Stund.   5
Nimm's lieber Alter auf dein Knie
Und denke mein wenns um dich schwebt
Wie es in Sympathien hie
Um mein verschwirbelt Hirngen lebt.
Geb Gott dir Lieb zu deinem Pantoffel   10
Ehr jede krüpliche Kartoffel
Erkenne jedes Dings Gestalt
Sein Leid und Freud Ruh und Gewalt
Und fühle wie die ganze Welt
Der große Himmel zusammen hält.   15
Dann du ein Zeichner, Colorist
Haltungs und Ausdrucks Meister bist.

An Schwager Kronos
In der Postchaise d 10 Oktbr 1774

Spude dich Kronos
Fort den rasselnden Trott!
Bergab gleitet der Weg
Ekles Schwindeln zögert
Mir vor die Stirne dein Haudern   5
Frisch, den holpernden
Stock, Wurzeln, Steine den Trott
Rasch in's Leben hinein.

Nun, schon wieder?
Den eratmenden Schritt   10
Mühsam Berg hinauf.
Auf denn! nicht träge denn!
Strebend und hoffend an.

Weit hoch herrlich der Blick
Rings ins Leben hinein 15
Vom Gebürg zum Gebürg
Über der ewige Geist
Ewigen Lebens ahndevoll.

Seitwärts des Überdachs Schatten 20
Zieht dich an
Und der Frischung verheißende Blick
Auf der Schwelle des Mädgens da.
Labe dich — mir auch Mädgen
Diesen schäumenden Trunk 25
Und den freundlichen Gesundheits Blick.

Ab dann frischer hinab
Sieh die Sonne sinkt!
Eh sie sinkt, eh mich faßt
Greisen im Moore Nebelduft, 30
Entzahnte Kiefer schnattern
Und das schlockernde Gebein

Trunknen vom letzten Strahl
Reiß mich, ein Feuermeer
Mir im schäumenden Aug, 35
Mich Geblendeten, Taumelnden,
In der Hölle nächtliches Tor

Töne Schwager dein Horn
Raßle den schallenden Trab
Daß der Orkus vernehme: ein Fürst kommt, 40
Drunten von ihren Sitzen
Sich die Gewaltigen lüften.

Neue Liebe neues Leben

Herz mein Herz was soll das geben?
Was bedränget dich so sehr?
Welch ein fremdes neues Leben!
Ich erkenne dich nicht mehr!
Weg ist alles was du liebtest, 5

Weg worum du dich betrübtest,
Weg dein Fleiß und deine Ruh,
Ach wie kamst du nur dazu.

Fesselt dich die Jugendblüte?
Diese liebliche Gestalt,   10
Dieser Blick voll Treu und Güte,
Mit unendlicher Gewalt?
Will ich rasch mich ihr entziehen
Mich ermannen ihr entfliehen;
Führet mich im Augenblick   15
Ach mein Weg zu ihr zurück.

Und an diesem Zauberfädgen
Das sich nicht zerreißen läßt
Hält das liebe lose Mädgen
Mich so wider willen fest.   20
Muß in ihrem Zauberkreise
Leben nun auf ihre Weise.
Die Verändrung ach wie groß!
Liebe liebe laß mich los.

An Belinden

Warum ziehst du mich unwiderstehlich
Ach in jene Pracht,
War ich guter Junge nicht so seelich
In der öden Nacht.

Heimlich in mein Zimmergen verschlossen   5
Lag im Mondenschein
Ganz von seinem Schauerlicht umflossen
Und ich dämmert ein

Träumte da von vollen goldnen Stunden
Ungemischter Lust   10
Hatte schon dein Liebes Bild empfunden
Tief in meiner Brust.

17

Bin ich's noch den du bei so viel Lichtern
An dem Spieltisch hältst
Oft so unerträglichen Gesichtern   15
Gegenüber stellst.

Reizender ist mir des Frühlings blüte
Nun nicht auf der Flur
Wo du Engel bist ist Lieb und Güte
Wo du bist Natur.   20

15. Junius 1775, aufm Zürichersee

Ich saug an meiner Nabelschnur
Nun Nahrung aus der Welt.
Und herrlich rings ist die Natur
Die mich am Busen hält.
Die Welle wieget unsern Kahn   5
Im Rudertakt hinauf
Und Berge Wolken angetan
Entgegnen unserm Lauf.

Aug mein Aug was sinkst du nieder
Goldne Träume kommt ihr wieder   10
Weg du Traum so Gold du bist
Hier auch Lieb und Leben ist.
Auf der Welle blinken
Tausend schwebende Sterne
Liebe Nebel trinken   15
Rings die türmende Ferne
Morgenwind umflügelt
Die beschattete Bucht
Und im See bespiegelt
Sich die reifende Frucht   20

Auf dem See

Und frische Nahrung, neues Blut
Saug' ich aus freier Welt;
Wie ist Natur so hold und gut,
Die mich am Busen hält!
Die Welle wieget unsern Kahn   5
Im Rudertakt hinauf,
Und Berge, wolkig himmelan,
Begegnen unserm Lauf.

Aug', mein Aug', was sinkst du nieder?
Goldne Träume kommt ihr wieder?   10
Weg, du Traum! so Gold du bist;
Hier auch Lieb' und Leben ist.

Auf der Welle blinken
Tausend schwebende Sterne,
Weiche Nebel trinken   15
Rings die türmende Ferne;
Morgenwind umflügelt
Die beschattete Bucht,
Und im See bespiegelt
Sich die reifende Frucht.   20

Im Herbst 1775

Fetter grüne du Laub
Das Rebengeländer
Hier mein Fenster herauf
Gedrängter quillet
Zwillingsbeeren, und reifet   5
Schneller und glänzend voller
Euch brütet der Mutter Sonne
Scheideblick, euch umsäuselt
Des holden Himmels
Fruchtende Fülle.   10
Euch kühlet des Monds
Freundlicher Zauberhauch
Und euch betauen, Ach!

Aus diesen Augen
Der ewig belebenden Liebe
Vollschwellende Tränen.

Two letter poems

Noch ein Wort eh ich schlafen gehe. Wie ich so in der Nacht gegen das
Fichtengebürg ritt; kam das Gefühl der Vergangenheit, meines Schicksaals,
und meiner Liebe über mich, und sang so bey mir selber:

Holde Lili warst so lang
All meine Lust und all mein Sang
Bist ach nun all mein Schmerz und doch
All mein Sang bist du noch.

*****

Nun aber und aber gute Nacht.

Gehab dich wohl bey den hundert Lichtern
Die dich umglänzen
Und all den Gesichtern
Die dich umschwänzen
Und umkredenzen.
Findst doch nur wahre Freud und Ruh
Bey Seelen grad und treu wie du

Wandrers Nachtlied

Der du von dem Himmel bist
Alle Freud und Schmerzen stillest,
Den der doppelt elend ist
Doppelt mit Erquickung füllest.
Ach ich bin des Treibens müde!
Was soll all die Qual und Lust.
Süßer Friede,
Komm ach komm in meine Brust!

Ein gleiches ✗ ✗ ✗

Über allen Gipfeln
Ist Ruh',
In allen Wipfeln
Spürest Du
Kaum einen Hauch;
Die Vögelein schweigen im Walde.
Warte nur! Balde
Ruhest du auch.

Warum gabst du uns die tiefen Blicke

Warum gabst du uns die tiefen Blicke
Unsre Zukunft ahndungsvoll zu schaun
Unsrer Liebe, unserm Erdenglücke
Wähnend selig nimmer hinzutraun?
Warum gabst uns Schicksal die Gefühle   5
Uns einander in das Herz zu sehn,
Um durch all die seltenen Gewühle
Unser wahr Verhältnis auszuspähn.

Ach so viele tausend Menschen kennen
Dumpf sich treibend kaum ihr eigen Herz,   10
Schweben zwecklos hin und her und rennen
Hoffnungslos in unversehnem Schmerz,
Jauchzen wieder wenn der schnellen Freuden
Unerwarte Morgenröte tagt.
Nur uns Armen liebevollen beiden   15
Ist das wechselseitge Glück versagt
Uns zu lieben ohn uns zu verstehen,
In dem Andern sehn was er nie war
Immer frisch auf Traumglück auszugehen
Und zu schwanken auch in Traumgefahr.   20

Glücklich den ein leerer Traum beschäftigt!
Glücklich dem die Ahndung eitel wär!
Jede Gegenwart und jeder Blick bekräftigt
Traum und Ahndung leider uns noch mehr.
Sag was will das Schicksal uns bereiten?   25

21

Sag wie band es uns so rein genau?
Ach du warst in abgelebten Zeiten
Meine Schwester oder meine Frau.

Kanntest jeden Zug in meinem Wesen,
Spähtest wie die reinste Nerve klingt,   30
Konntest mich mit Einem Blicke lesen
Den so schwer ein sterblich Aug durchdringt.
Tropftest Mäßigung dem heißen Blute,
Richtetest den wilden irren Lauf,
Und in deinen Engelsarmen ruhte   35
Die zerstörte Brust sich wieder auf,
Hieltest zauberleicht ihn angebunden
Und vergaukeltest ihm manchen Tag.
Welche Seligkeit glich jenen Wonnestunden,
Da er dankbar dir zu Füßen lag.   40
Fühlt sein Herz an deinem Herzen schwellen,
Fühlte sich in deinem Auge gut,
Alle seine Sinnen sich erhellen
Und beruhigen sein brausend Blut.

Und von allem dem schwebt ein Erinnern   45
Nur noch um das ungewisse Herz
Fühlt die alte Wahrheit ewig gleich im Innern,
Und der neue Zustand wird ihm Schmerz.
Und wir scheinen uns nur halb beseelet
Dämmernd ist um uns der hellste Tag.   50
Glücklich daß das Schicksal das uns quälet
Uns doch nicht verändern mag.

Seefahrt

Tag lang Nacht lang stand mein Schiff befrachtet,
Günstger Winde harrend saß mit treuen Freunden
Mir Geduld und guten Mut erzechend
Ich im Hafen.

Und sie wurden mit mir ungeduldig   5
Gerne gönnen wir die schnellste Reise
Gern die hohe Fahrt dir. Güterfülle

Wartet drüben in den Welten deiner
Wird rückkehrendem in unsern Armen
Lieb und Preis dir.   10

Und am frühen Morgen wards Getümmel
Und dem Schlaf entjauchzt uns der Matrose
Alles wimmelt alles lebet webet
Mit dem ersten Segenshauch zu schiffen.

Und die Segel blühen in dem Hauche   15
Und die Sonne lockt mit Feuerliebe
Ziehn die Segel, ziehn die hohen Wolken
Jauchzen an dem Ufer alle Freunde
Hoffnungslieder nach im Freudetaumel
Reisefreuden wähnend wie des Einschiffmorgens 20
Wie der ersten hohen Sternennächte.

Aber Gottgesandte Wechselwinde treiben
Seitwärts ihn der vorgesteckten Fahrt ab
Und er scheint sich ihnen hinzugeben
Strebet leise sie zu überlisten,   25
Treu dem Zweck auch auf dem schiefen Wege.

Aber aus der dumpfen grauen Ferne
Kündet leise wandelnd sich der Sturm an
Drückt die Vögel nieder auf's Gewässer
Drückt der Menschen schwellend Herze nieder.   30
Und er kommt. — Vor seinem starren Wüten,
Streckt der Schiffer weis die Segel nieder,
Mit dem angsterfüllten Balle spielen
Wind und Wellen.

Und an jenem Ufer drüben stehen   35
Freund und lieben, beben auf dem Festen:
Ach warum ist er nicht hiergeblieben
Ach der Sturm! Verschlagen weg vom Glücke
Soll der Gute so zu Grunde gehen?
Ach er sollte! Ach er könnte! Götter!   40

Doch er stehet männlich an dem Steuer
Mit dem Schiffe spielen Wind und Wellen

23

Wind und Wellen nicht mit seinem Herzen.
Herrschend blickt er auf die grimme Tiefe,
Und vertrauet scheiternd oder landend
Seinen Göttern.

45

Eis-Lebens Lied

Sorglos über die Fläche weg
Wo vom kühnsten Wager die Bahn
Dir nicht vorgegraben du siehst
Mache dir selber Bahn! —
Stille Liebgen mein Herz
Krachts gleich brichts doch nicht,
Brichts gleich, bricht nicht mit dir

ⴲ ⵣ ⵝ   Erlkönig

Wer reitet so spät durch Nacht und Wind?
Es ist der Vater mit seinem Kind;
Er hat den Knaben wohl in dem Arm,
Er faßt ihn sicher, er hält ihn warm.

Mein Sohn, was birgst du so bang dein Gesicht? —
Siehst, Vater, du den Erlkönig nicht?
Den Erlenkönig mit Kron' und Schweif? —
Mein Sohn, es ist ein Nebelstreif. —

5

»Du liebes Kind, komm, geh mit mir;
Gar schöne Spiele spiel' ich mit dir,
Manch bunte Blumen sind an dem Strand,
Meine Mutter hat manch gülden Gewand.« —

10

Mein Vater, mein Vater, und hörest du nicht,
Was Erlenkönig mir leise verspricht? —
Sei ruhig, bleibe ruhig, mein Kind;
In dürren Blättern säuselt der Wind. —

15

»Willst, feiner Knabe, du mit mir gehn?
Meine Töchter sollen dich warten schön:

Meine Töchter führen den nächtlichen Reihn,
Und wiegen und tanzen und singen dich ein.« —   20

Mein Vater, mein Vater, und siehst du nicht dort
Erlkönigs Töchter am düstern Ort? —
Mein Sohn, mein Sohn, ich seh' es genau;
Es scheinen die alten Weiden so grau. —

»Ich liebe dich, mich reizt deine schöne Gestalt;   25
Und bist du nicht willig, so brauch' ich Gewalt!«
Mein Vater, mein Vater, jetzt faßt er mich an!
Erlkönig hat mir ein Leids getan! —

Dem Vater grauset's, er reitet geschwind,
Er hält in Armen das ächzende Kind,   30
Erreicht den Hof mit Mühe und Not;
In seinen Armen das Kind war tot.

Vor Gericht

Von wem ich's habe das sag ich euch nicht
Das Kind in meinem Leib,
Pfui speit ihr aus die Hure da!
Bin doch ein ehrlich Weib.

Mit wem ich mich traute das sag ich euch nicht   5
Mein Schatz ist lieb und gut
Trägt er eine goldne Kett am Hals
Trägt er einen strohernen Hut.

Soll Spott und Hohn getragen sein
Trag ich allein den Hohn,   10
Ich kenn' ihn wohl, er kennt mich wohl
Und Gott weiß auch davon.

Herr Pfarrer und Herr Amtmann ihr
Ich bitt laßt mich in Ruh,
Es ist mein Kind und bleibt mein Kind,   15
Ihr gebt mir ja nichts dazu.

Grenzen der Menschheit

Wenn der uralte,
Heilige Vater
Mit gelassener Hand
Aus rollenden Wolken
Segnende Blitze   5
Über die Erde sä't,
Küss' ich den letzten
Saum seines Kleides,
Kindliche Schauer
Treu in der Brust.   10

Denn mit Göttern
Soll sich nicht messen
Irgend ein Mensch.
Hebt er sich aufwärts,
Und berührt   15
Mit dem Scheitel die Sterne,
Nirgends haften dann
Die unsichern Sohlen,
Und mit ihm spielen
Wolken und Winde.   20

Steht er mit festen,
Markigen Knochen
Auf der wohlgegründeten,
Dauernden Erde;
Reicht er nicht auf,   25
Nur mit der Eiche
Oder der Rebe
Sich zu vergleichen.

Was unterscheidet
Götter von Menschen?   30
Daß viele Wellen
Vor jenen wandeln,
Ein ewiger Strom:
Uns hebt die Welle,
Verschlingt die Welle,   35
Und wir versinken.

Ein kleiner Ring
Begrenzt unser Leben,
Und viele Geschlechter
Reihen sich dauernd   40
An ihres Daseins
Unendliche Kette.

Das Göttliche

Edel sei der Mensch,
Hülfreich und gut!
Denn das allein
Unterscheidet ihn
Von allen Wesen,   5
Die wir kennen.

Heil den unbekannten
Höhern Wesen,
Die wir ahnden!
Ihnen gleiche der Mensch   10
Sein Beispiel lehr' uns
Jene glauben.

Denn unfühlend
Ist die Natur:
Es leuchtet die Sonne   15
Über Bös' und Gute,
Und dem Verbrecher
Glänzen wie dem Besten
Der Mond und die Sterne.

Wind und Ströme,   20
Donner und Hagel
Rauschen ihren Weg,
Und ergreifen,
Vorüber eilend,
Einen um den andern.   25

Auch so das Glück
Tappt unter die Menge,

Faßt bald des Knaben
Lockige Unschuld,
Bald auch den kahlen   30
Schuldigen Scheitel.

Nach ewigen, ehrnen,
Großen Gesetzen,
Müssen wir alle
Unseres Daseins   35
Kreise vollenden.

Nur allein der Mensch
Vermag das Unmögliche:
Er unterscheidet,
Wählet und richtet;   40
Er kann dem Augenblick
Dauer verleihen.

Er allein darf
Dem Guten lohnen,
Den Bösen strafen;   45
Heilen und retten
Alles Irrende, Schweifende
Nützlich verbinden.

Und wir verehren
Die Unsterblichen,   50
Als wären sie Menschen,
Täten im Großen,
Was der Beste im Kleinen
Tut oder möchte.

Der edle Mensch   55
Sei hülfreich und gut!
Unermüdet schaff' er
Das Nützliche, Rechte,
Sei uns ein Vorbild
Jener geahndeten Wesen!   60

Mignon

Kennst du das Land, wo die Citronen blühn,
Im dunkeln Laub die Gold-Orangen glühn,
Ein sanfter Wind vom blauen Himmel weht,
Die Myrte still und hoch der Lorbeer steht,
Kennst du es wohl?
          Dahin! Dahin   5
Möcht' ich mit dir, o mein Geliebter, ziehn.

Kennst du das Haus? Auf Säulen ruht sein Dach,
Es glänzt der Saal, es schimmert das Gemach,
Und Marmorbilder stehn und sehn mich an:
Was hat man dir, du armes Kind, getan?   10
Kennst du es wohl?
          Dahin! Dahin
Möcht' ich mit dir, o mein Beschützer, ziehn.

Kennst du den Berg, und seinen Wolkensteg?
Das Maultier sucht im Nebel seinen Weg;
In Höhlen wohnt der Drachen alte Brut;   15
Es stürzt der Fels und über ihn die Flut.
Kennst du ihn wohl?
          Dahin! Dahin
Geht unser Weg! o Vater, laß uns ziehn!

Römische Elegien

III

Laß dich, Geliebte, nicht reu'n, daß du mir so schnell dich ergeben!
    Glaub' es, ich denke nicht frech, denke nicht niedrig von dir.
Vielfach wirken die Pfeile des Amor: einige ritzen,
    Und vom schleichenden Gift kranket auf Jahre das Herz.
Aber mächtig befiedert, mit frisch geschliffener Schärfe   5
    Dringen die andern ins Mark, zünden behende das Blut.
In der heroischen Zeit, da Götter und Göttinnen liebten,
    Folgte Begierde dem Blick, folgte Genuß der Begier.
Glaubst du, es habe sich lange die Göttin der Liebe besonnen,
    Als im Idäischen Hain einst ihr Anchises gefiel?   10

Hätte Luna gesäumt, den schönen Schäfer zu küssen;
  O, so hätt' ihn geschwind, neidend, Aurora geweckt.
Hero erblickte Leandern beim lauten Fest, und behende
  Stürzte der Liebende sich heiß in die nächtliche Flut.
Rhea Sylvia wandelt, die fürstliche Jungfrau, der Tiber   15
  Wasser zu schöpfen, hinab, und sie ergreifet der Gott.
So erzeugte die Söhne sich Mars! — Die Zwillinge tränket
  Eine Wölfin, und Rom nennt sich die Fürstin der Welt.

V

Froh empfind' ich mich nun auf klassischem Boden begeistert;
  Vor- und Mitwelt spricht lauter und reizender mir.
Hier befolg' ich den Rat, durchblättre die Werke der Alten
  Mit geschäftiger Hand, täglich mit neuem Genuß.
Aber die Nächte hindurch hält Amor mich anders beschäftigt;   5
  Werd' ich auch halb nur gelehrt, bin ich doch doppelt beglückt.
Und belehrt' ich mich nicht, indem ich des lieblichen Busens
  Formen spähe, die Hand leite die Hüften hinab?
Dann versteh' ich den Marmor erst recht; ich denk' und vergleiche,
  Sehe mit fühlendem Aug', fühle mit sehender Hand.   10
Raubt die Liebste denn gleich mir einige Stunden des Tages,
  Gibt sie Stunden der Nacht mir zur Entschädigung hin.
Wird doch nicht immer geküßt, es wird vernünftig gesprochen,
  Überfällt sie der Schlaf, lieg ich und denke mir viel.
Oftmals hab' ich auch schon in ihren Armen gedichtet   15
  Und des Hexameters Maß, leise, mit fingernder Hand,
Ihr auf den Rücken gezählt, sie atmet in lieblichem Schlummer
  Und es durchglühet ihr Hauch mir bis ins tiefste die Brust.
Amor schüret indes die Lampe und denket der Zeiten,
  Da er den nämlichen Dienst seinen Triumvirn getan.   20

IX

Herbstlich leuchtet die Flamme vom ländlich geselligen Herde,
  Knistert und glänzet, wie rasch! sausend vom Reisig empor.
Diesen Abend erfreut sie mich mehr; denn eh' noch zur Kohle
  Sich das Bündel verzehrt, unter die Asche sich neigt,
Kommt mein liebliches Mädchen. Dann flammen Reisig und Scheite,   5

Und die erwärmte Nacht wird uns ein glänzendes Fest.
  Morgen frühe geschäftig verläßt sie das Lager der Liebe,
  Weckt aus der Asche behend Flammen aufs Neue hervor.
Denn vor andern verlieh der Schmeichlerin Amor die Gabe,
  Freude zu wecken, die kaum still wie zu Asche versank.   10

Klein ist unter den Fürsten...

Klein ist unter den Fürsten Germaniens freilich der meine;
  Kurz und schmal ist sein Land, mäßig nur, was er vermag.
Aber so wende nach innen, so wende nach außen die Kräfte
  Jeder; da wär's ein Fest, Deutscher mit Deutschen zu sein.
Doch was priesest du Ihn, den Taten und Werke verkünden?   5
  Und bestochen erschien deine Verehrung vielleicht;
Denn mir hat er gegeben, was Große selten gewähren,
  Neigung, Muße, Vertraun, Felder und Garten und Haus.
Niemand braucht' ich zu danken als ihm, und Manches bedurft' ich,
  Der ich mich auf den Erwerb schlecht, als ein Dichter, verstand.   10
Hat mich Europa gelobt, was hat mir Europa gegeben?
  Nichts! Ich habe, wie schwer! meine Gedichte bezahlt.
Deutschland ahmte mich nach, und Frankreich mochte mich lesen.
  England! freundlich empfingst du den zerrütteten Gast.
Doch was fördert es mich, daß auch sogar der Chinese   15
  Malet, mit ängstlicher Hand, Werthern und Lotten auf Glas?
Niemals frug ein Kaiser nach mir, es hat sich kein König
  Um mich bekümmert, und Er war mir August und Mäzen.

Metamorphose der Tiere

Wagt ihr, also bereitet, die letzte Stufe zu steigen
Dieses Gipfels, so reicht mir die Hand und öffnet den freien
Blick ins weite Feld der Natur. Sie spendet die reichen
Lebensgaben umher, die Göttin; aber empfindet
Keine Sorge wie sterbliche Fraun um ihrer Gebornen   5
Sichere Nahrung; ihr ziemet es nicht: denn zwiefach bestimmte
Sie das höchste Gesetz, beschränkte jegliches Leben,
Gab ihm gemess'nes Bedürfnis, und ungemessene Gaben,
Leicht zu finden, streute sie aus, und ruhig begünstigt
Sie das muntre Bemühn der vielfach bedürftigen Kinder;   10
Unerzogen schwärmen sie fort nach ihrer Bestimmung.

Zweck sein selbst ist jegliches Tier, vollkommen entspringt es
Aus dem Schoß der Natur und zeugt vollkommene Kinder.
Alle Glieder bilden sich aus nach ew'gen Gesetzen
Und die seltenste Form bewahrt im Geheimen das Urbild.   15
So ist jeglicher Mund geschickt die Speise zu fassen
Welche dem Körper gebührt, es sei nun schwächlich und zahnlos
Oder mächtig der Kiefer gezahnt, in jeglichem Falle
Fördert ein schicklich Organ den übrigen Gliedern die Nahrung.
Auch bewegt sich jeglicher Fuß, der lange, der kurze,   20
Ganz harmonisch zum Sinne des Tiers und seinem Bedürfnis.
So ist jedem der Kinder die volle reine Gesundheit
Von der Mutter bestimmt: denn alle lebendigen Glieder
Widersprechen sich nie und wirken alle zum Leben.
Also bestimmt die Gestalt die Lebensweise des Tieres   25
Und die Weise zu leben sie wirkt auf alle Gestalten
Mächtig zurück. So zeiget sich fest die geordnete Bildung,
Welche zum Wechsel sich neigt durch äußerlich wirkende Wesen.
Doch im Innern befindet die Kraft der edlern Geschöpfe
Sich im heiligen Kreise lebendiger Bildung beschlossen.   30
Diese Grenzen erweitert kein Gott, es ehrt die Natur sie:
Denn nur also beschränkt war je das Vollkommene möglich.

Doch im Inneren scheint ein Geist gewaltig zu ringen,
Wie er durchbräche den Kreis, Willkür zu schaffen den Formen
Wie dem Wollen; doch was er beginnt, beginnt er vergebens.   35
Denn zwar drängt er sich vor zu diesen Gliedern, zu jenen,
Stattet mächtig sie aus, jedoch schon darben dagegen
Andere Glieder, die Last des Übergewichtes vernichtet
Alle Schöne der Form und alle reine Bewegung.
Siehst du also dem einen Geschöpf besonderen Vorzug   40
Irgend gegönnt, so frage nur gleich, wo leidet es etwa
Mangel anderswo, und suche mit forschendem Geiste,
Finden wirst du sogleich zu aller Bildung den Schlüssel.
Denn so hat kein Tier, dem sämtliche Zähne den obern
Kiefer umzäunen, ein Horn auf seiner Stirne getragen,   45
Und daher ist den Löwen gehörnt der ewigen Mutter
Ganz unmöglich zu bilden und böte sie alle Gewalt auf;
Denn sie hat nicht Masse genug die Reihen der Zähne
Völlig zu pflanzen und auch Geweih und Hörner zu treiben.

Dieser schöne Begriff von Macht und Schranken, von Willkür   50
Und Gesetz, von Freiheit und Maß, von beweglicher Ordnung,
Vorzug und Mangel, erfreue dich hoch; die heilige Muse
Bringt harmonisch ihn dir, mit sanftem Zwange belehrend.
Keinen höhern Begriff erringt der sittliche Denker,
Keinen der tätige Mann, der dichtende Künstler; der Herrscher,   55
Der verdient es zu sein, erfreut nur durch ihn sich der Krone.
Freue dich, höchstes Geschöpf, der Natur, du fühlest dich fähig
Ihr den höchsten Gedanken, zu dem sie schaffend sich aufschwang,
Nachzudenken. Hier stehe nun still und wende die Blicke
Rückwärts, prüfe, vergleiche, und nimm vom Munde der Muse   60
Daß du schauest, nicht schwärmst, die liebliche volle Gewißheit.

Sonette

Sich in erneutem Kunstgebrauch zu üben,
   Ist heil'ge Pflicht, die wir dir auferlegen:
   Du kannst dich auch, wie wir, bestimmt bewegen
Nach Tritt und Schritt, wie es dir vorgeschrieben.

Denn eben die Beschränkung läßt sich lieben,
   Wenn sich die Geister gar gewaltig regen;   5
   Und wie sie sich denn auch gebärden mögen,
Das Werk zuletzt ist doch vollendet blieben.

So möcht' ich selbst in künstlichen Sonetten,
   In sprachgewandter Maßen kühnem Stolze,
   Das Beste, was Gefühl mir gäbe, reimen;   10

Nur weiß ich hier mich nicht bequem zu betten,
   Ich schneide sonst so gern aus ganzem Holze,
   Und müßte nun doch auch mitunter leimen.

*****

Natur und Kunst sie scheinen sich zu fliehen,
Und haben sich, eh' man es denkt, gefunden;
Der Widerwille ist auch mir verschwunden,
Und beide scheinen gleich mich anzuziehen.

Es gilt wohl nur ein redliches Bemühen!   5
Und wenn wir erst in abgemess'nen Stunden
Mit Geist und Fleiß uns an die Kunst gebunden,
Mag frei Natur im Herzen wieder glühen.

So ist's mit aller Bildung auch beschaffen:
Vergebens werden ungebundne Geister   10
Nach der Vollendung reiner Höhe streben.

Wer Großes will muß sich zusammenraffen;
In der Beschränkung zeigt sich erst der Meister,
Und das Gesetz nur kann uns Freiheit geben.

Dauer im Wechsel

Hielte diesen frühen Segen
Ach, nur Eine Stunde fest!
Aber vollen Blütenregen
Schüttelt schon der laue West.
Soll ich mich des Grünen freuen   5
Dem ich Schatten erst verdankt?
Bald wird Sturm auch das zerstreuen
Wenn es falb im Herbst geschwankt.

Willst du nach den Früchten greifen,
Eilig nimm dein Teil davon!   10
Diese fangen an zu reifen
Und die andern keimen schon;
Gleich mit jedem Regengusse,
Ändert sich dein holdes Tal,
Ach, und in demselben Flusse   15
Schwimmst du nicht zum zweitenmal.

Du nun selbst! Was felsenfeste
Sich vor dir hervorgetan,
Mauern siehst du, siehst Paläste
Stets mit andern Augen an.   20
Weggeschwunden ist die Lippe,
Die im Kusse sonst genas,
Jener Fuß, der an der Klippe
Sich mit Gemsenfreche maß,

34

Jene Hand, die gern und milde 25
Sich bewegte wohlzutun.
Das gegliederte Gebilde,
Alles ist ein andres nun.
Und was sich, an jener Stelle,
Nun mit deinem Namen nennt, 30
Kam herbei wie eine Welle
Und so eilt's zum Element.

Laß den Anfang mit dem Ende
Sich in Eins zusammen ziehn!
Schneller als die Gegenstände 35
Selber dich vorüberfliehn.
Danke, daß die Gunst der Musen
Unvergängliches verheißt,
Den Gehalt in deinem Busen
Und die Form in deinem Geist. 40

Hatem

Locken, haltet mich gefangen
In dem Kreise des Gesichts!
Euch geliebten braunen Schlangen
Zu erwidern hab' ich nichts.

Nur dies Herz, es ist von Dauer,
Schwillt in jugendlichstem Flor; 5
Unter Schnee und Nebelschauer
Rast ein Ätna dir hervor.

Du beschämst wie Morgenröte
Jener Gipfel ernste Wand,
Und noch einmal fühlet Hatem 10
Frühlingshauch und Sommerbrand.

Schenke her! Noch eine Flasche!
Diesen Becher bring' ich ihr!
Findet sie ein Häufchen Asche,
Sagt sie: »Der verbrannte mir.« 15

Suleika

Ach, um deine feuchten Schwingen,
West, wie sehr ich dich beneide:
Denn du kannst ihm Kunde bringen,
Was ich in der Trennung leide.

Die Bewegung deiner Flügel   5
Weckt im Busen stilles Sehnen;
Blumen, Augen, Wald und Hügel
Stehn bei deinem Hauch in Tränen.

Doch dein mildes sanftes Wehen
Kühlt die wunden Augenlider;   10
Ach, für Leid müßt' ich vergehen,
Hofft' ich nicht zu sehn ihn wieder.

Eile denn zu meinem Lieben,
Spreche sanft zu seinem Herzen;
Doch vermeid' ihn zu betrüben   15
Und verbirg ihm meine Schmerzen.

Sag' ihm, aber sag's bescheiden:
Seine Liebe sei mein Leben,
Freudiges Gefühl von beiden
Wird mir seine Nähe geben.   20

Einlaß

Huri

Heute steh' ich meine Wache
Vor des Paradieses Tor,
Weiß nicht grade, wie ich's mache,
Kommst mir so verdächtig vor!

Ob du unsern Mosleminen   5
Auch recht eigentlich verwandt?
Ob dein Kämpfen, dein Verdienen
Dich ans Paradies gesandt?

Zählst du dich zu jenen Helden?
Zeige deine Wunden an,   10
Die mir Rühmliches vermelden,
Und ich führe dich heran.

Dichter

Nicht so vieles Federlesen!
Laß mich immer nur herein:
Denn ich bin ein Mensch gewesen,   15
Und das heißt ein Kämpfer sein.

Schärfe deine kräft'gen Blicke!
Hier! — durchschaue diese Brust,
Sieh der Lebenswunden Tücke,
Sieh der Liebeswunden Lust.   20

Und doch sang ich gläubigerweise:
Daß mir die Geliebte treu,
Daß die Welt, wie sie auch kreise,
Liebevoll und dankbar sei.

Mit den Trefflichsten zusammen   25
Wirkt' ich, bis ich mir erlangt,
Daß mein Nam' in Liebesflammen
Von den schönsten Herzen prangt.

Nein! du wählst nicht den Geringern;
Gib die Hand! daß Tag für Tag   30
Ich an deinen zarten Fingern
Ewigkeiten zählen mag.

Urworte. Orphisch

ΔΑΙΜΩΝ, Dämon

Wie an dem Tag, der dich der Welt verliehen,
Die Sonne stand zum Gruße der Planeten,
Bist alsobald und fort und fort gediehen,
Nach dem Gesetz wonach du angetreten.
So mußt du sein, dir kannst du nicht entfliehen,   5
So sagten schon Sibyllen, so Propheten;
Und keine Zeit und keine Macht zerstückelt
Geprägte Form die lebend sich entwickelt.

ΤΥΧΗ, Das Zufällige

Die strenge Grenze doch umgeht gefällig
Ein Wandelndes, das mit und um uns wandelt;   10
Nicht einsam bleibst du, bildest dich gesellig,
Und handelst wohl so wie ein andrer handelt:
Im Leben ist's bald hin- bald widerfällig,
Es ist ein Tand und wird so durchgetandelt.
Schon hat sich still der Jahre Kreis geründet,   15
Die Lampe harrt der Flamme die entzündet.

ΕΡΩΣ, Liebe

Die bleibt nicht aus! — Er stürzt vom Himmel nieder,
Wohin er sich aus alter Öde schwang,
Er schwebt heran auf luftigem Gefieder
Um Stirn und Brust den Frühlingstag entlang,   20
Scheint jetzt zu fliehn, vom Fliehen kehrt er wieder,
Da wird ein Wohl im Weh, so süß und bang.
Gar manches Herz verschwebt im Allgemeinen,
Doch widmet sich das edelste dem Einen.

ΑΝΑΓΚΗ, Nötigung

Da ist's denn wieder wie die Sterne wollten: 25
Bedingung und Gesetz und aller Wille
Ist nur ein Wollen, weil wir eben sollten,
Und vor dem Willen schweigt die Willkür stille;

Das Liebste wird vom Herzen weggescholten,
Dem harten Muß bequemt sich Will' und Grille.   30
So sind wir scheinfrei denn nach manchen Jahren
Nur enger dran als wir am Anfang waren.

ΕΛΠΙΣ, Hoffnung

Doch solcher Grenze, solcher ehrnen Mauer
Höchst widerwärt'ge Pforte wird entriegelt,
Sie stehe nur mit alter Felsendauer!   35
Ein Wesen regt sich leicht und ungezügelt:
Aus Wolkendecke, Nebel, Regenschauer
Erhebt sie uns, mit ihr, durch sie beflügelt,
Ihr kennt sie wohl, sie schwärmt durch alle Zonen;
Ein Flügelschlag — und hinter uns Äonen!   40

St. Nepomuks Vorabend
Carlsbad den 15. Mai 1820

Lichtlein schwimmen auf dem Strome,
Kinder singen auf der Brücken,
Glocke, Glöckchen fügt vom Dome
Sich der Andacht, dem Entzücken.
Lichtlein schwinden, Sterne schwinden;   5
Also lös'te sich die Seele
Unsres Heil'gen, nicht verkünden
Durft' er anvertraute Fehle.

Lichtlein schwimmet! spielt ihr Kinder!
Kinder-Chor, o! singe, singe!   10
Und verkündiget nicht minder
Was den Stern zu Sternen bringe.

Parabase

Freudig war, vor vielen Jahren,
Eifrig so der Geist bestrebt,
Zu erforschen, zu erfahren,
Wie Natur im Schaffen lebt.

39

Und es ist das ewig Eine,   5
Das sich vielfach offenbart;
Klein das Große, groß das Kleine,
Alles nach der eignen Art.
Immer wechselnd, fest sich haltend,
Nah und fern und fern und nah;   10
So gestaltend, umgestaltend —
Zum Erstaunen bin ich da.

Trilogie der Leidenschaft

An Werther

Noch einmal wagst du, vielbeweinter Schatten,
Hervor dich an das Tageslicht,
Begegnest mir auf neu beblümten Matten
Und meinen Anblick scheust du nicht.
Es ist als ob du lebtest in der Frühe,   5
Wo uns der Tau auf Einem Feld erquickt,
Und nach des Tages unwillkommner Mühe
Der Scheidesonne letzter Strahl entzückt;
Zum Bleiben ich, zum Scheiden du, erkoren,
Gingst du voran — und hast nicht viel verloren.   10

Des Menschen Leben scheint ein herrlich Los:
Der Tag, wie lieblich, so die Nacht, wie groß!
Und wir gepflanzt in Paradieses Wonne,
Genießen kaum der hocherlauchten Sonne,
Da kämpft sogleich verworrene Bestrebung   15
Bald mit uns selbst und bald mit der Umgebung;
Keins wird vom andern wünschenswert ergänzt,
Von außen düstert's, wenn es innen glänzt,
Ein glänzend Äußres deckt mein trüber Blick,
Da steht es nah — und man verkennt das Glück.   20

Nun glauben wir's zu kennen! Mit Gewalt
Ergreift uns Liebreiz weiblicher Gestalt:
Der Jüngling, froh wie in der Kindheit Flor
Im Frühling tritt als Frühling selbst hervor,
Entzückt, erstaunt, wer dies ihm angetan?   25

40

Er schaut umher, die Welt gehört ihm an.
In's Weite zieht ihn unbefangene Hast,
Nichts engt ihn ein, nicht Mauer, nicht Palast;
Wie Vögelschar an Wäldergipfeln streift,
So schwebt auch er, der um die Liebste schweift,   30
Er sucht vom Äther, den er gern verläßt,
Den treuen Blick und dieser hält ihn fest.

Doch erst zu früh und dann zu spät gewarnt,
Fühlt er den Flug gehemmt, fühlt sich umgarnt,
Das Wiedersehn ist froh, das Scheiden schwer,   35
Das Wieder-Wiedersehn beglückt noch mehr
Und Jahre sind im Augenblick ersetzt;
Doch tückisch harrt das Lebewohl zuletzt.

Du lächelst, Freund, gefühlvoll wie sich ziemt:
Ein gräßlich Scheiden machte dich berühmt;   40
Wir feierten dein kläglich Mißgeschick,
Du ließest uns zu Wohl und Weh zurück;
Dann zog uns wieder ungewisse Bahn
Der Leidenschaften labyrinthisch an;
Und wir verschlungen wiederholter Not,   45
Dem Scheiden endlich — Scheiden ist der Tod!
Wie klingt es rührend wenn der Dichter singt,
Den Tod zu meiden, den das Scheiden bringt!
Verstrickt in solche Qualen halbverschuldet
Geb' ihm ein Gott zu sagen was er duldet.   50

Elegie

    Und wenn der Mensch in seiner Qual verstummt,
    Gab mir ein Gott zu sagen was ich leide.

Was soll ich nun vom Wiedersehen hoffen,
Von dieses Tages noch geschloss'ner Blüte
Das Paradies, die Hölle steht dir offen;
Wie wankelsinnig regt sich's im Gemüte! —
Kein Zweifeln mehr! Sie tritt an's Himmelstor,   5
Zu Ihren Armen hebt sie dich empor.

—

So warst du denn im Paradies empfangen
Als wärst du wert des ewig schönen Lebens;
Dir blieb kein Wunsch, kein Hoffen, kein Verlangen,
Hier war das Ziel des innigsten Bestrebens,   10
Und in dem Anschaun dieses einzig Schönen
Versiegte gleich der Quell sehnsüchtiger Tränen.

Wie regte nicht der Tag die raschen Flügel,
Schien die Minuten vor sich her zu treiben!
Der Abendkuß, ein treu verbindlich Siegel: 15
So wird es auch der nächsten Sonne bleiben.
Die Stunden glichen sich in zartem Wandern
Wie Schwestern zwar, doch keine ganz den andern.

Der Kuß der letzte, grausam süß, zerschneidend
Ein herrliches Geflecht verschlungner Minnen.   20
Nun eilt, nun stockt der Fuß die Schwelle meidend,
Als trieb ein Cherub flammend ihn von hinnen;
Das Auge starrt auf düstrem Pfad verdrossen,
Es blickt zurück, die Pforte steht verschlossen.

Und nun verschlossen in sich selbst, als hätte   25
Dies Herz sich nie geöffnet, selige Stunden
Mit jedem Stern des Himmels um die Wette
An ihrer Seite leuchtend nicht empfunden;
Und Mißmut, Reue, Vorwurf, Sorgenschwere
Belasten's nun in schwüler Atmosphäre.   30

Ist denn die Welt nicht übrig? Felsenwände
Sind sie nicht mehr gekrönt von heiligen Schatten?
Die Ernte reift sie nicht? Ein grün Gelände
Zieht sich's nicht hin am Fluß durch Busch und Matten?
Und wölbt sich nicht das überweltlich Große   35
Gestaltenreiche, bald gestaltenlose?

Wie leicht und zierlich, klar und zart gewoben,
Schwebt, Seraph gleich, aus ernster Wolken Chor,
Als glich es ihr, am blauen Äther droben,
Ein schlank Gebild aus lichtem Duft empor: 40
So sahst du sie in frohem Tanze walten
Die Lieblichste der lieblichsten Gestalten.

Doch nur Momente darfst dich unterwinden
Ein Luftgebild statt ihrer fest zu halten;
In's Herz zurück, dort wirst du's besser finden,   45
Dort regt sie sich in wechselnden Gestalten;
Zu Vielen bildet Eine sich hinüber,
So tausendfach, und immer immer lieber.

Wie zum Empfang sie an den Pforten weilte
Und mich von dannauf stufenweis beglückte;   50
Selbst nach dem letzten Kuß mich noch ereilte,
Den letztesten mir auf die Lippen drückte:
So klar beweglich bleibt das Bild der Lieben,
Mit Flammenschrift, in's treue Herz geschrieben.

In's Herz, das fest wie zinnenhohe Mauer   55
Sich ihr bewahrt und sie in sich bewahret,
Für sie sich freut an seiner eignen Dauer,
Nur weiß von sich, wenn sie sich offenbaret,
Sich freier fühlt in so geliebten Schranken
Und nur noch schlägt, für alles ihr zu danken.   60

War Fähigkeit zu lieben, war Bedürfen
Von Gegenliebe weggelöscht, verschwunden;
Ist Hoffnungslust zu freudigen Entwürfen,
Entschlüssen, rascher Tat sogleich gefunden!
Wenn Liebe je den Liebenden begeistet,   65
Ward es an mir auf's lieblichste geleistet;

Und zwar durch sie! — Wie lag ein innres Bangen
Auf Geist und Körper, unwillkommner Schwere:
Von Schauerbildern rings der Blick umfangen
Im wüsten Raum beklommner Herzensleere;   70
Nun dämmert Hoffnung von bekannter Schwelle,
Sie selbst erscheint in milder Sonnenhelle.

Dem Frieden Gottes, welcher euch hienieden
Mehr als Vernunft beseliget — wir lesen's —
Vergleich' ich wohl der Liebe heitern Frieden   75
In Gegenwart des allgeliebten Wesens;
Da ruht das Herz und nichts vermag zu stören
Den tiefsten Sinn, den Sinn ihr zu gehören.

In unsers Busens Reine wogt ein Streben,
Sich einem höhern, reinern, unbekannten,   80
Aus Dankbarkeit freiwillig hinzugeben,
Enträtselnd sich den ewig Ungenannten;
Wir heißen's: fromm sein! — Solcher seligen Höhe
Fühl' ich mich teilhaft, wenn ich vor ihr stehe.

Vor ihrem Blick, wie vor der Sonne Walten,   85
Vor ihrem Atem, wie vor Frühlingslüften,
Zerschmilzt, so längst sich eisig starr gehalten,
Der Selbstsinn tief in winterlichen Grüften;
Kein Eigennutz, kein Eigenwille dauert,
Vor ihrem Kommen sind sie weggeschauert.   90

Es ist als wenn sie sagte: »Stund um Stunde
Wird uns das Leben freundlich dargeboten,
Das Gestrige ließ uns geringe Kunde,
Das Morgende, zu wissen ist's verboten;
Und wenn ich je mich vor dem Abend scheute,   95
Die Sonne sank und sah noch was mich freute.

Drum tu' wie ich und schaue, froh verständig,
Dem Augenblick in's Auge! Kein Verschieben!
Begegn' ihm schnell, wohlwollend wie lebendig,
Im Handeln sei's, zur Freude, sei's dem Lieben;   100
Nur wo du bist sei alles, immer kindlich,
So bist du alles, bist unüberwindlich.«

Du hast gut reden, dacht' ich, zum Geleite
Gab dir ein Gott die Gunst des Augenblickes,
Und jeder fühlt an deiner holden Seite   105
Sich Augenblicks den Günstling des Geschickes;
Mich schreckt der Wink von dir mich zu entfernen,
Was hilft es mir so hohe Weisheit lernen!

Nun bin ich fern! Der jetzigen Minute
Was ziemt denn der? Ich wüßt' es nicht zu sagen;   110
Sie bietet mir zum Schönen manches Gute,
Das lastet nur, ich muß mich ihm entschlagen;
Mich treibt umher ein unbezwinglich Sehnen,
Da bleibt kein Rat als grenzenlose Tränen.

So quellt denn fort! und fließet unaufhaltsam;   115
Doch nie geläng's die innre Glut zu dämpfen!
Schon rast's und reißt in meiner Brust gewaltsam,
Wo Tod und Leben grausend sich bekämpfen.
Wohl Kräuter gäb's, des Körpers Qual zu stillen;
Allein dem Geist fehlt's am Entschluß und Willen,   120

Fehlt's am Begriff: wie sollt' er sie vermissen?
Er wiederholt ihr Bild zu tausendmalen.
Das zaudert bald, bald wird es weggerissen,
Undeutlich jetzt und jetzt im reinsten Strahlen;
Wie könnte dies geringstem Troste frommen,   125
Die Ebb' und Flut, das Gehen wie das Kommen?

—

Verlaßt mich hier, getreue Weggenossen!
Laßt mich allein am Fels, in Moor und Moos;
Nur immer zu! euch ist die Welt erschlossen,
Die Erde weit, der Himmel hehr und groß;   130
Betrachtet, forscht, die Einzelheiten sammelt,
Naturgeheimnis werde nachgestammelt.

Mir ist das All, ich bin mir selbst verloren,
Der ich noch erst den Göttern Liebling war;
Sie prüften mich, verliehen mir Pandoren,   135
So reich an Gütern, reicher an Gefahr;
Sie drängten mich zum gabeseligen Munde,
Sie trennen mich, und richten mich zu Grunde.

Aussöhnung

Die Leidenschaft bringt Leiden! — Wer beschwichtigt
Beklommnes Herz das allzuviel verloren?
Wo sind die Stunden, überschnell verflüchtigt?
Vergebens war das Schönste dir erkoren!
Trüb' ist der Geist, verworren das Beginnen;   5
Die hehre Welt wie schwindet sie den Sinnen!

45

Da schwebt hervor Musik mit Engelschwingen,
Verflicht zu Millionen Tön' um Töne,
Des Menschen Wesen durch und durch zu dringen,
Zu überfüllen ihn mit ew'ger Schöne: 10
Das Auge netzt sich, fühlt im höhern Sehnen
Den Götter-Wert der Töne wie der Tränen.

Und so das Herz erleichtert merkt behende
Daß es noch lebt und schlägt und möchte schlagen,
Zum reinsten Dank der überreichen Spende   15
Sich selbst erwidernd willig darzutragen.
Da fühlte sich — o daß es ewig bliebe! —
Das Doppel-Glück der Töne wie der Liebe.

Im ernsten Beinhaus war's

Im ernsten Beinhaus war's wo ich beschaute
    Wie Schädel Schädeln angeordnet paßten;
    Die alte Zeit gedacht' ich, die ergraute.
Sie stehn in Reih' geklemmt, die sonst sich haßten,
    Und derbe Knochen die sich tödlich schlugen   5
    Sie liegen kreuzweis, zahm allhier zu rasten.
Entrenkte Schulterblätter! was sie trugen
    Fragt niemand mehr, und zierlich tät'ge Glieder,
    Die Hand, der Fuß zerstreut aus Lebensfugen.
Ihr Müden also lagt vergebens nieder,   10
    Nicht Ruh im Grabe ließ man euch, vertrieben
    Seid ihr herauf zum lichten Tage wieder,
Und niemand kann die dürre Schale lieben,
    Welch herrlich edlen Kern sie auch bewahrte.
    Doch mir Adepten war die Schrift geschrieben,   15
Die heil'gen Sinn nicht jedem offenbarte,
    Als ich in Mitten solcher starren Menge
    Unschätzbar herrlich ein Gebild gewahrte,
Daß in des Raumes Moderkält und Enge
    Ich frei und wärmefühlend mich erquickte,   20
    Als ob ein Lebensquell dem Tod entspränge.
Wie mich geheimnisvoll die Form entzückte!
    Die gottgedachte Spur, die sich erhalten!
    Ein Blick der mich an jenes Meer entrückte

Das flutend strömt gesteigerte Gestalten. 25
   Geheim Gefäß! Orakelsprüche spendend,
   Wie bin ich wert dich in der Hand zu halten?
Dich höchsten Schatz aus Moder fromm entwendend,
   Und in die freie Luft, zu freiem Sinnen,
   Zum Sonnenlicht andächtig hin mich wendend. 30
Was kann der Mensch im Leben mehr gewinnen
   Als daß sich Gott-Natur ihm offenbare?
   Wie sie das Feste läßt zu Geist verrinnen,
   Wie sie das Geisterzeugte fest bewahre.

Chinesisch-deutsche Jahres- und Tageszeiten

I

Sag was könnt' uns Mandarinen,
Satt zu herrschen, müd zu dienen,
Sag was könnt' uns übrig bleiben,
Als in solchen Frühlingstagen
Uns des Nordens zu entschlagen 5
Und am Wasser und im Grünen
Fröhlich trinken, geistig schreiben,
Schal' auf Schale, Zug in Zügen?

VIII

Dämmrung senkte sich von oben,
Schon ist alle Nähe fern;
Doch zuerst emporgehoben
Holden Lichts der Abendstern!
Alles schwankt in's Ungewisse 5
Nebel schleichen in die Höh;
Schwarzvertiefte Finsternisse
Wiederspiegelnd ruht der See.

Nun im östlichen Bereiche
Ahnd' ich Mondenglanz und Glut, 10
Schlanker Weiden Haargezweige
Scherzen auf der nächsten Flut.
Durch bewegter Schatten Spiele

Zittert Luna's Zauberschein,
Und durch's Auge schleicht die Kühle   15
Sänftigend in's Herz hinein.

IX

Nun weiß man erst was Rosenknospe sei,
Jetzt da die Rosenzeit vorbei;
Ein Spätling noch am Stocke glänzt
Und ganz allein die Blumenwelt ergänzt.

Wenn im Unendlichen dasselbe...

Wenn im Unendlichen dasselbe
Sich wiederholend ewig fließt,
Das tausendfältige Gewölbe
Sich kräftig in einander schließt;
Strömt Lebenslust aus allen Dingen,   5
Dem kleinsten wie dem größten Stern,
Und alles Drängen, alles Ringen
Ist ewige Ruh' in Gott dem Herrn.

Dornburger Gedichte

Dem aufgehenden Vollmonde
Dornburg, August 1828

Willst du mich sogleich verlassen!
Warst im Augenblick so nah!
Dich umfinstern Wolkenmassen
Und nun bist du gar nicht da.

Doch du fühlst wie ich betrübt bin,   5
Blickt dein Rand herauf als Stern!
Zeugest mir daß ich geliebt bin,
Sei das Liebchen noch so fern.

So hinan denn! hell und heller,
Reiner Bahn, in voller Pracht!   10
Schlägt mein Herz auch schmerzlich schneller,
Überselig ist die Nacht.

Dornburg, September 1828

Früh wenn Tal, Gebirg und Garten
Nebelschleiern sich enthüllen,
Und dem sehnlichsten Erwarten
Blumenkelche bunt sich füllen;

Wenn der Äther, Wolken tragend,   5
Mit dem klaren Tage streitet,
Und ein Ostwind, sie verjagend,
Blaue Sonnenbahn bereitet;

Dankst du dann, am Blick dich weidend,
Reiner Brust der Großen, Holden,   10
Wird die Sonne, rötlich scheidend,
Rings den Horizont vergolden.

In ein Album

Würd' ein künstlerisch Bemühen
Rosenbüsche, wie sie blühen,
Rosenkrone, wie sie leuchtet,
Hell, von Morgentau befeuchtet,
Diesen Blättern anvertrauen,   5
Würdest du dein Bildnis schauen;
Wie's der Sommergarten hegt,
Bleibt's in unsrer Brust geprägt.

Am längsten Tage 1831

NOTES TO THE POEMS

The secondary works quoted and referred to below are listed, with their abbreviations, in the Bibliography (p. xxiii). Several of these contain detailed linguistic commentary, which has here been kept to a minimum.

An den Schlaf   1767   (p. 1)

This early poem sets impulse against obstacle: the lover's (natural) desire and the awkward (conventional) presence of the girl's mother. He asks Sleep to help his plans.

The poem is more playful than serious. It springs from a 'culture of wit' prevalent in German writing in the 1760s, especially in Leipzig, where Goethe was a student. Before finding his own poetic voice – he is only eighteen – he follows the literary fashion.

So the poem is about impulse and obstacle in a second sense: any individual way the young man might write about love is pre-empted and blocked by the convention of the day, which prescribes the poetic mode, mood and vocabulary. Love is called 'Amor' and lovers become 'shepherds', as in classical idylls; sleep too is personified as a classical figure (Morpheus, Hypnos) with the attributes of poppy (= opium) and wings.

But did the poet have a real emotion to *be* pre-empted and blocked? Or did he perhaps imagine one for the purposes of writing a fashionable poem? Exercises in an established mode are the almost unavoidable way for young poets to begin. The fascination with poetry – with words, rhythms, images, rhymes – and the even profounder impulse to be a poet, are often there before a compelling poetic substance. Within these limits, Goethe is already handling his means with structural elegance (the deft double 'sinking' in the last two lines) and rhythmic aptness (the address to Sleep in ll. 1 and 19). Serious referents for the motifs the beginner is here playing with will come later. Two decades on, a love-affair of a different order will be watched over by Amor, appropriately in the classical setting of the *Roman Elegies*; and as part of the tragic action of *Faust*, the hero passes Gretchen a sleeping potion to give to her mother which proves fatal.

lines 20 and 23: *schlaf'* and *sink'* are present-tense (or K1) subjunctives; in both cases = 'may she...'

Die Nacht   1768 (p. 1)

Another early poem, which embodies similar poetic issues. Night and a silent wood are the setting for a mini-drama of love: this is the place where 'she' is staying. The final line, in a way typical of Rococo erotic verse, uses 'night' in the limited meaning of 'sexual intercourse'. Yet the poem begins with the lover *glad* to leave his beloved's cottage and wander about stealthily ('mit verhülltem Tritt', l. 3) in the dark, enjoying a night-mood more specific and more absorbing than is strictly necessary to prepare the typical Rococo punch-line. Nature is beginning to exert a distinctive fascination, and to stimulate the observer's sensibility – e.g. the visual effect of 'bricht die Nacht der Eichen' in l. 5 (Goethe is a powerfully visual poet).

So despite, once again, stylised classical names – 'Luna' for the moon, 'Zephirs' for the breezes – the poem begins to evoke a credible situation and responses ('Schauer...schmelzen macht', ll. 9f). And although the culminating exclamations of l. 13 – 'Freude! Wollust! kaum zu fassen' – are meant to suggest how much greater the longed-for sexual satisfaction would be (to be precise, a thousand times greater than the ones that are the poem's substance), still, night in the woods has a self-sufficient interest; the more so since readers in the 1760s, familiar with the poetic conventions of the day, will have virtually discounted the 'witty' ending in advance as predictable.

An Behrisch, 3. Ode   1767 (p. 2)

In 1767, Goethe's friend Ernst Wolfgang Behrisch lost his position as private tutor in a noble family and left Leipzig. Goethe addressed three odes to him, of lament, enouragement and advice. This one first recommends the stoic principle of avoiding emotional involvements (even friendship) so as not to be hurt when expectations fail (sts. 1-3); warns of the viciousness of human envy, presumably what was responsible for the rumours that damaged Behrisch's reputation with his employer (sts. 4-6); laments the friends' separation (st. 7); urges Behrisch to make a clean break with Leipzig and not hark back disablingly to their friendship (sts. 8-9); for Behrisch's new freedom (by the end of the poem his dismissal begins to look more like an escape) will be a comfort to the friend he is leaving behind him still in prison – i.e., Goethe has one more year of his university course to complete!

The poem thus treats a real episode in the lives of two people. There was no conventional poetic form that would accommodate its specific features, so language and layout had to improvise a response to them. It is true there are familiar rhetorical terms and contrasts – the inconstant earth (l. 4), the spring/winter contrast (st. 2), the rejected consolations of love and friendship (ll. 9f); the turning cycle of the year as a chariot wheel with flying spokes and a smoking-hot axle (last two stanzas) which may be specific borrowings from the Pindaric tradition (see on *Wandrers Sturmlied*). Yet there is also inventiveness in language and imagery: 'sorgenverwiegend', 'elendtragend' – 'rocking away cares', 'supporting misery' (ll. 9f) – and the dramatic picture of envy as a lynx waiting to pounce from a high rock (st. 4).

More important, instead of regular metre and rhyme, the poem is organised in sense-units which are made clear by the line-breaks. Statements are given the space to make their point emphatically, even a touch solemnly – but then, in the poet's young experience, this *is* a solemn moment. A background influence here is Friedrich Gottlieb Klopstock, whose Odes originally used heavily accentuated stanza-patterns taken over from Greek and Latin poetry and then moved to increasingly 'free' patterns of his own devising, but kept the strong accentuation to reinforce meaning and emotion. This ode, though, is noticeably more terse than Klopstock's normally are. The free form is suited to the theme, his friend's escape from a hostile conventional society. Goethe's poem is thus a small escape of his own. These tentative formal beginnings soon take off as a powerful new mode for much grander utterances.

Heidenröslein c.1771 (p. 3)

The poem is obviously in simple 'folksong' style, but it has mysteries, including whether Goethe actually wrote it. For cultivated people in the eighteenth and early nineteenth century, folksong possessed the values of naturalness and simplicity. Famous collections date from then – Thomas Percy's *Reliques of Ancient English Poetry* (1765), Achim von Arnim and Clemens Brentano's *Des Knaben Wunderhorn* (1806-8). Folksong was an interest Goethe shared with his friend Herder during their time in Strasbourg in 1770-1.

What did all this contribute to Goethe's poem? The phrase 'Röslein auf der Heiden', seems to come from a folksong in an old collection (by Paul von der Aelst, 1602) in Herder's possession; though the words Goethe added – 'Röslein, Röslein, Röslein rot' – build up the refrain into a stronger rhythmic incantation. Herder's essay of 1773, *Über Ossian und die Lieder alter Völker*, quotes an 'old German' example very like Goethe's poem (Eibl 1, 124f) and he talks about the effect achieved by leaving out the definite article – 'Knabe brach', 'Röslein stach' – which is to give the nouns more 'substance and personality'. This is a trick Goethe's poem uses, though the text Herder is quoting does not. So was it Goethe's own 'Heidenröslein' that Herder was quoting from memory? And if so, had Goethe led him to think it was an authentic folksong, as James Macpherson had persuaded the public of the day that his *Songs of Ossian* were based on authentic Gaelic poetry? Or did

Goethe know and adapt that (otherwise unidentified) 'old German' example? Or had he perhaps collected an authentic one himself on his wanderings in the Alsace countryside listening, as he said, to the songs of old grannies ('Müttergens')?

Authentic folksongs, like those in the *Reliques* and the *Wunderhorn*, are usually long, often rambling and repetitious. Goethe's poem, by contrast, has terse phrasing and an economical narrative that spring from the concentration on a single brief encounter. Is that the whole story, and is the poem a literal narration of this real encounter, 'the story of a rape' (Eibl 1, 830)? If so, 'ich breche dich' would be a threat of male violence that was actually uttered ('brechen', though, is a normal verb for picking a flower) and 'ich steche dich' would be a counter-threat of female fingernails. Or is the poem a fable, as Herder called that 'old German' song, compressing into a symbolic encounter a whole unhappy love-history, in which the boy takes the initiative and the girl suffers emotional and perhaps social injury, yet also leaves a lasting mark on him? 'Daß du *ewig* denkst an mich' suggests permanent guilt rather than just a scratched face. In social terms, such a fable would amount to just as serious an accusation against the male actor as the now (fashionably?) assumed account of rape. In literary terms, the question is whether a poem of this kind must, or can, be read in the same way as a realistic short story, or whether it has other, distinctive, means of its own.

Maifest 1771 [Revised in 1789 as **Mailied**] (p. 4)

Folksong simplicity again, but one that manages to capture a whole natural complex and also to include the human speaker in it as an integral part of nature. He is not just a detached observer, introducing things he has seen and reflections they give rise to. In fact he scarcely *describes* anything. Instead the poem is dominated by exclamations of wonder, delight and gratitude – no lyric better bears out D.H. Lawrence's remark that a poem is the prolonging of an exclamation.

That does not mean *Maifest* is just so many disjointed cries of pleasure. It has a triadic structure, an underlying logic and even a nature philosophy of its own. It perceives nature first as a single luminous whole, the sun above and the earth beneath. That may seem too basic to be worth stating; yet stating the fundamentals of life is one function of poets. Who else will? And the strength of feeling the opening lines express makes them elemental, not just elementary. In sts. 2 and 3 instances of life and growth are linked as deeply related phenomena by the way they all share the same verb of compulsive process, 'dringen'. Blossom, birdsong and human feeling are products of a common natural force.

In st. 4 that force is addressed as 'love' – the first sign that the phenomena around the speaker are not simply self-sufficient. Clearly 'love' here means more than just his feeling for the young woman (st. 6), though this human love is as much part of the grand force as is the love which he imagines the lark and the flower feeling for their common environment of air (an instance of the 'pathetic fallacy'?). If the human form of this all-pervading love inspires song, then poetry too is ultimately rooted in nature. The mutual love of the speaker and the girl is a channel through which the same forces flow that shape the outside world he delights in. The old idea of the beloved as the poet's Muse is recreated from fresh materials and given a deeper grounding in the world around them.

It has been said the poem evokes 'the divine as manifested in nature' (Eibl 1, 841), though the divine is never mentioned as such. The intensity of celebration might suggest rather that nature is itself being raised to a divine status – something rather different. And does the poet's delight in the visible world really presuppose an 'experience of alienation', however familiar that may since have become as a motif of modern culture (**MA** 1, i, 837)? On the formal side, the underlying structure of three phases, each with three stanzas, looks like a conscious calculation. Or can formal symmetry be spontaneously generated? Further evidence is offered by *Auf dem See*.

Mir schlug das Herz   1771   (p. 6 & 7)
[Revised for 1789 *Collected Works* as **Willkomm und Abschied** in later editions: **Willkommen...**]

This poem, with its drastic shift from wild energy to tender feeling, might be called 'heroic' or 'mock-heroic love lyric', but would probably then be the only instance in its class. First there is the impetuous departure and the ride through darkness and dangers (are they real or imaginary? seriously or humorously described?). Then at the poem's mid-point, which is the moment of arrival, seeing the beloved transforms the tone into a sudden serenity This has been called a 'decline in vigour of language' (Boyle, 113), but is surely a necessary change of pace if the young woman is not to be ridden down by the pounding rhythms. These are now reined in, though without any change in the formal metre – the movement of language within a fixed metrical pattern can be infinitely varied. A horse might be thought of as a symbol of sexual potency, although here it is first of all a necessary means of transport. (As Freud said, 'Sometimes a cigar is just a cigar'.) But if horse and riding are read in that sexually symbolic way – even at the literal level they certainly embody the initiative of the male lover – then they meet their match in the compelling gentleness of the girl's presence. The emotion with which the poem ends is a different kind of exhilaration from the adventurous excitement of the opening.

When Goethe revised the poem, he plainly tried to tone down the extremes of both movement and emotion in the poem's first half and to get a less drastic contrast with the milder mood of the second half, while still keeping the final climax where love is reaffirmed despite the suffering it can cause. We can guess what the mature man disapproved of in the poem his younger self had written: a hero storming off to battle in line 2 must have seemed ill suited to a lover's tryst. But does the revision 'Es war getan fast eh gedacht' sound excited *enough*? Again, to call his courage 'tausendfach*er*' than the thousand dangers of the night (l. 14) was to break the logical bounds of language; while to say that his mind was a consuming fire and his heart was melting with ardour inside him (ll. 15f) was way over the top. Yet is caution a good criterion for poetry? And when if not in youth and in love is the language of feeling allowed to be immoderate? These fine extremes needed to be preserved as part of the human record. Luckily they were.

More fundamentally, it looks as if some notion of symmetry suggested reshaping the whole situation, so that the man, who arrives first, is also the one to depart. But this neatness is gained at the price of transforming the original poem, and with it presumably the truth of the experience, real or imaginary, that inspired it. The change is simple on the surface but has intricate consequences. Keeping the same rhyme-words but attributing the sentiments to a different partner means that there is a change in the logic of what is said about the emotions, and in the authority with which it is said. The tears which in version 1 the speaker feels in his own eyes ('ich [...] mit nassem Blick') are answered by his own words of exuberant reaffirmation, 'Und doch, welch Glück...'. It is a different matter with the tears which in version 2 , though he is already going away, he somehow knows are in her eyes ('du [...] mit nassem Blick'). This alters the sense of the outwardly unchanged conclusion that follows. Is the reaffirmation still his? Or is it now (more logically) hers? Or does it belong to them both? However one reads it, the affirmative ending no longer has its original authority of a man speaking, under the pressure of emotion, for himself. What is more, the new ending to the last stanza – 'Doch ach, schon mit der Morgensonne' – suggests they have spent the night together. The poem becomes what in medieval poetry was called a 'Tagelied', a song of lovers parting at dawn to avoid discovery. The real young woman who Goethe declared, admittedly long afterwards, had inspired his poem is thus shown in a damaging social light. Does that make it justifiable to speak, as Klaus Weimar does (p. 31), of a dishonest ending and the 'incompetence' of writers in interpreting and adapting their own texts?

Protest as we may, reworking poems is a common practice of poets; indeed, they find it hard to leave well alone. Wordsworth, for instance, went on all his life rewriting his long poem *The Prelude*, which was meant as an autobiographical record of 'the growth of a poet's mind'. Part of the 'growth' is thus contained, less straightforwardly than the sub-title meant, not in what the poem tells us about the poet's youth, but in the changes he went on making to the way he wanted his youth to be seen. Some of these changes have been regarded as marking not the growth, but the decline of a poet's mind. *Willkommen und Abschied* shows some of the possible aims of revision, and raises large questions of the possible gain and loss – aesthetic, ethical, even historical – that are at stake.

Comparison: Robert Browning, *Night meeting*.

Gretchen am Spinnrade   some time in the 1770s   (p. 8)

At the centre of *Faust* Part I is Faust's love affair with Gretchen, which ends with her facing execution for murdering their child. The infanticide theme was probably brought home to Goethe as lawyer, lover, man, and writer by the real case of Susanne Margarete Brandt, who was tried and executed in Frankfurt am Main in 1771-2. Goethe finished this play-within-a-play – it virtually hijacks the traditional Faust action for its own self-sufficient purpose – very promptly, as if under a compulsion that did not extend to the rest of the work. (*Faust* Part I took him three more decades to complete.) Compulsion is certainly suggested by the quality of the writing, both verse and prose, which is as moving in its power and directness as anything Goethe ever wrote. His extraordinary empathy into Gretchen's mind, passion and suffering created the most memorable woman figure in German literature.

Gretchen's yearning for Faust combines a folksong simplicity with the personal truth of her situation. What is virtually a song (it was movingly set as one by Schubert) makes up a whole brief scene, typical of the lyrical style of the earliest-written parts of Goethe's play. If it were a free-standing poem, it would class as a 'Rollengedicht', the construction from within of a named person's thoughts and feelings (cf. *Prometheus*). Even as a role in an actual drama, it is heightened beyond Gretchen's other speeches, in both the intensity of her emotion and the clarity of her awareness.

Goethe never published the scene in its original form, which is found in the so-called 'Urfaust' (not an early version of *Faust*, but a transcript of the scenes that Goethe had written by 1775, made by a Weimar lady, presumably after Goethe had read them to the Court). For the 1808 *Faust I* Goethe largely left well alone, but he did change l. 33 to read 'Mein *Busen* drängt sich...' That still presses hard against the proprieties of Goethe's day, but is less expressive than the line it replaced: his first instinct, as usual, had been uncannily right. For this is not just a romantic affair but a love that will produce a child, with tragic consequences. That ultimate result is starkly foreshadowed in 'Schoß'; while the broken rhythm of the original line and Gretchen's tormented exclamation 'Gott' – no trivial exclamation for a young woman of her background and beliefs – carry an even stronger charge of desire.

Wandrers Sturmlied   1774   (p. 9)

This is a wild and wind-blown poem. Years later in *Dichtung und Wahrheit* Goethe called it, somewhat dismissively, 'Halbunsinn', and recalled how he sang it to himself while plodding through the storm on one of the walks for which he gained a reputation among his friends – hiking for pleasure not then being normal – as 'the wanderer'. In an accompanying letter at the time (to Friedrich Heinrich Jacobi, 31 August 1774) he said it was 'eine Ode, zu der Melodie und Kommentar nur der Wanderer in der Not findet'. Did that mean you had to have been similarly drenched and stormed on to understand it? Yet the poem conveys what an encounter with the elements feels like, rain, hail, snow, mud, with only the human being's 'innere Wärme' – his physical warmth, but also his morale – to set against them. The mode is 'dithyrambic', i.e., enthusiastic and celebratory in the manner of the Greek poet Pindar, who wrote odes in honour of victorious athletes and charioteers. But there are differences. For one thing, Goethe is celebrating his own guardian spirit or 'Genius' and the divinities that inhabit the world he draws comfort and inspiration from: a private destiny, not a public triumph. For another, it is not so certain he will triumph at all. It takes a lot of effort to battle on in the teeth of the elements, his confidence waxes and wanes, and it is touch and go whether he will get through. He is well aware of this, and there are touches of wry self-irony that nicely counterpoint the grand Pindaric gestures. The mixing in of colloquial phrases and the almost out-of-breath speech rhythms are part of the parodic fun. All this keeps his feet metaphorically on the ground, even though at times he feels borne up by his Genius (st. 2). Still, the humour does not altogether undo the grand manner, in a way it enriches and strengthens it. This would-be hero has one more resource in his struggles – he can take himself humorously as well as seriously. That saves him from the potentially tragic tension of do-or-die effort. At the close it looks as if he will make it, though only just; his humble dwelling is in sight, and if the guardian spirit will only grant one last bit of extra heat for his boiler, he will be home, though not dry.

Behind all this is the question: how does modern man – the modern creative individual – measure up not just to the elements but to the ancients?

The poem moves in associative leaps and allusions, so it needs some commentary to link them in an argument:

stanza 1: If only (this is throughout a question, not a certainty) his Genius

57

does not abandon him, he will successfully ride the weather like the lark high above him.

stanza 2: If only...(the same hope is repeated), then he will be wafted over the mud. (Deukalion in Greek mythology, like Noah, survived a flood. The Python was a monster engendered by the flood; the god Apollo killed it.)

stanzas 3 and 4: Wings now not to waft, but to warm and comfort him.

stanzas 5 and 6: An invocation to the poetic graces (Charitinnen). The speaker's progress – 'wandeln' , then 'schweben', and especially 'Göttergleich', making up, emphatically, the last line of both stanzas – marks a crest of confidence. 'Sohn des Wassers und der Erde' = mud.

stanza 7: With such support, will he lack the courage to get him back home, when a mere swarthy peasant is clearly managing, with only the expectation of wine (Vater Bromius = Bacchus, the god of wine) and a fire to keep his spirits up?

stanza 8: much of the inspiration of the times *is* only Dutch courage, unlike the inner fire of Pindar's day and the inspiration that Apollo (god of poetry) can still provide.

stanza 9: Apollo will not think much of anyone – presumably, any poet – who lacks the inner warmth. 'Neidgetroffen' reads as if it refers to Apollo's 'princely gaze' – but why should the god feel 'envy'? Commentators have suggested that it is the wanderer who is smitten by envy ('dich...neidgetroffen'), i.e., if Apollo's approving gaze falls elsewhere: specifically, on the cedar's vigorous green growth, a symbol for the spontaneous creative force in which the wanderer is found wanting. That would tidy the sense, but is a counter-intuitive reading of the syntax.

stanza 10: The wanderer may lack fire, but at least his song is flowing like the rain. So why has he not long since invoked Jupiter as god of rain (pluvius)? The Castalian spring (on the poetic mountain Parnassus – if you drank from it, you became a poet) is not much ('ein Nebenbach') beside the torrential rainfall he is being thoroughly drenched by ('mich fassend deckst').

stanza 11: This is not the way the god inspired those poets of tranquil Greek idyll, Anakreon and Theocritus.

stanza 12: The exciting climax of the chariot race was the real subject for poetry (Apollo and poetic creation are not named again, but are present by implication in the scene evoked, contrasting with modern subjects) and Pindar rose to the occasion with the heat of his own inspiration, his soul 'glowed' in response to the 'dangers'.

'Yes, glowed', the wanderer says to himself, ruefully, ironically, rousing his storm-bedraggled self one last time to compete with legendary Greek fire: 'I'll be lucky if I'm granted just enough modern fire to get me back home'.

Prometheus 1774 (p. 12)

A classic 'Rollengedicht', but drawn from an actual drama on Prometheus that Goethe abandoned. The two-act fragment is preserved; the poem takes over in changed form some phrases from it. (Goethe similarly adapted a passage from another abandoned drama, *Mahomet*, as a lyrical poem, though not this time a 'Rollengedicht'.)

The title tells us we are hearing a mythological figure speak. But myths commonly exist in different versions – over time, each myth became so to speak a basic story with optional extras. So when a poet uses a myth, we have to note which of its elements are plainly present; which are missing; which are in some way implied in the background; and what new elements or emphases of his own the poet may have added.

Prometheus was a kind of demi-god, a Titan (which makes l. 30 puzzling) who made the first human beings from clay. Later he stole fire from the gods for them when Zeus had withheld it; he also cheated Zeus over religious sacrifices, by using only the skin and bones of the animals so that human beings got the better bits. To punish his offences, Zeus chained him to a rock in the Caucasus where an eagle daily hacked at his liver, which grew again at night. So Prometheus is an obvious symbol of human cunning, creativity, independence, and stoic suffering. In Goethe's poem, independence is the central theme.

There could hardly be more defiant speech-gestures than in that opening: stark imperatives (i.e., orders, addressed to a god, and the top god at that) and a peremptory statement, the more brusque because 'mußt' has no 'du'with it, that Zeus can do nothing to Prometheus and his house. What about Zeus' conventional attribute, the thunderbolt, with which he could surely destroy any structure? Does 'Hütte' perhaps mean a dwelling place in a wider, less fragile sense, the habitation that human beings have made for themselves on earth with their skills, customs, cultures (see Klaus Weimar, p. 91)? Prometheus has indeed already called the whole earth his own. Human independence becomes possible if the gods really are the poorest thing under the sun – 'under', because they are only kept going by the more foolish of human beings, those still immature ('Kinder') and those too poor in resources of their own ('Bettler'), both of whom hope for divine help.

Stanzas 3 and 4 are a flashback to the time when Prometheus shared these hopes, but got no help and so had to achieve everything himself. There is pride (l. 29ff), esp. in his 'heilig glühend Herz', which recalls the crucial inner heat *Wandrers Sturmlied* speaks of. It is the more vehemently expressed because the need was then so great, as the emotive phrasing (ll. 28 and 38ff) makes clear.

Stanza 5 draws the conclusion that Prometheus owes nothing to the gods, and everything, his own efforts apart, to the way time and fate matured him. Fate is a force that in Greek mythology was higher than the gods, not shaped or decreed by them; and st. 6 scornfully rejects the alternative of despair that might have followed when Prometheus lost his faith in divine power and benevolence.

Instead, back in the present now and looking to the future, the final stanza declares that the human forms Prometheus creates in his own image will know the full range of sufferings and joys and will, especially, pay no heed to Zeus just – the last line is an emphatic full stop – like him.

There are problems with the match of myth and poem. After or alongside the original humanity, which Prometheus in Goethe's version presumably did not make, and which stood/stands in awe of the gods (cf. the present tense 'nähret' in l. 15) is there now to be a second human race? That is a tall order, so some critics retreat to the position that Prometheus is a symbol for the Artist, who creates a new race only in his works; but that sacrifices much of Prometheus' mythic power and the story's expressive potential. If his defiance and disbelief are only to be passed on to fictional beings, leaving real mankind as gullible and deceived as ever, the poem becomes a much less radical, not to say a trivial statement. Prometheus' reference to 'his' earth (l. 6) surely suggests far more than a private artistic world; it sounds like a sweeping humanist assertion of a new earth, if not a new heaven. New starts are nothing new in myth – in fact they are a regular thing, following after floods and incarnations, revelations and fresh covenants. This would be a non-religious one.

Is it not contradictory, though, to use a monologue addressed to a god as a means of denying the gods' existence? Or can a myth or poem imply, philosophically, the non-existence outside it of things that are represented as realities inside it? The monologue and its speaker, after all, are constructed by the poet, who may see further than his character and imply more than his character can see or say. For Prometheus, the gods' total failure to help him means they are a miserable crew. That, however, might merely be the last of his illusions. The conclusion might equally well be that they are not there at all. In Goethe's dramatic fragment, they unambiguously do exist, for Prometheus is Zeus' son. The poem, though, is a different work. It contains no divine response, whether by voice or action. Certainly there is no thought that Prometheus will be punished by Zeus: that central element of the myth is very conspicuously absent. In the opening stanza, indeed, Prometheus denies that Zeus has any power to get at him or the things he has made.

None of this makes Prometheus' vehemence any less plausible. It is a truism that God often seems to be more dramatically real to the passionate atheist than to the biddable believer. Nor does it mean that Goethe entered any the less into the character's situation; a myth only needs to offer the poet points of contact, openings for empathy. The dramatic power of Goethe's language is the measure of how completely empathy was achieved.

Note incidentally that Prometheus' disappointed expectations of divine help have specifically Christian echoes ('erbarmen' in l. 28; 'Beladenen' in l. 40). These words hardly make sense in the Greek context. And might that closing expression of defiance through the stubborn assertion of a physical posture – 'Hier sitz ich' – just possibly be meant to recall the words Luther used at the Diet of Worms to assert his necessary independence against the established church: 'Hier steh ich und kann nicht anders'?

Ganymed 1774   (p. 14)

Ganymede is another myth, of a Trojan shepherd-boy whom Zeus' eagle carried off to be cup-bearer to the gods on Olympus. Starting with the earliest MS collection of his poems (c.1778) and through all his subsequent published editions, Goethe placed *Ganymed* immediately after *Prometheus*. Conclusions have often been drawn: that the poems were two of a kind (both are indeed dramatic monologues and both invoke myth) so perhaps their themes were being set against each other, with Ganymed's intense devotion and happy elevation to Olympus meant to balance, perhaps even to take back, Prometheus' rebellion against the gods. These conclusions may even have been shared by Goethe – that is, by Goethe as the editor of his own work, someone not quite identical with the poet who wrote the poems several years before; and by Goethe the autobiographer when, from an even greater distance in time and so even less identical with his young self, he presented the two poems as expressions of diametrically opposed impulses: self-realisation (*Verselbstung*) and the yielding up of self (*Entselbstigung*).

The emotions in *Ganymed* are certainly at the opposite extreme from what Prometheus feels: delight, love, an impulse to join with a higher loving power, which grows out of an ecstatic perception of the beauties of the world. The speaker responds as a lover, spring 'glows at' him (again that motif of heat and light), plant life literally presses on him (ll. 4f; 13f). Two full stanzas evoke what his senses register; each is followed by a two-line expression of yearning for closer contact with the beauty all round him. The only uncertainty is: how can he answer the loving call, and in what direction should he move to achieve union? The concluding stanza combines both elements – ecstasy and action, attraction and response; nature continues to take the initiative, the clouds descend to bear him up to the 'all-loving father'. The ecstatic language rises to new heights at the same time as he does.

The match with myth is more problematic than in *Prometheus*. The

Ganymede myth is only a slight narrative, and has none of this emotional intensity. The boy had no near-mystical experience of nature. Nor did he aspire to higher things, he was simply carried off, to serve the company of the gods rather than to be embraced by a single god – though some Latin poets, e.g. Martial, do assume Zeus' interest in Ganymed was sexual, as a change from his many heterosexual escapades. But that is not what is meant by 'Alliebender Vater' (l. 32), with its obvious Christian ring; and the clouds that have replaced Zeus' eagle recall the Christian iconography of Bodily Assumptions. Title apart, the poem does not name the boy, the god, Olympus, or anything else that would localise it in Greece or in myth.

So there is not much left of what was already not much of a myth, and nothing to parallel the rich substance of *Prometheus*, however much that other story may have been adapted. Are the two poems then really a pair? Why, even before pairing them, did Goethe call this poem 'Ganymed' at all when the links with the legend are so slight? Does the title really announce a version of the myth, and was Goethe consciously writing one? Or did he use the title – perhaps as an afterthought – to catch at a distant analogy, and thereby actually give far more substance to the myth than the myth gave to the poem? That would make *Ganymed* 'mythic' in a strong sense, rather than just 'mythological': that is to say, it does not so much borrow an ancient story as renew and transform it by infusing into it an intense modern experience – new wine in old bottles. For modern the speaker's experience decidedly is. It is part of the eighteenth century's celebration of nature which needed no licensing by ancient Greece, and indeed could hardly have found a model there. For the Greeks famously did not make much of the natural world as a theme, did not ncessarily even have (so Schiller argued in his essay *Über naive und sentimentalische Dichtung*) a conception of 'nature' in the modern sense at all. Schiller put it in an elegant contrast: the Greeks had 'natural feeling', we now have a 'feeling for nature'. That is our loss, not theirs, for the new feeling is essentially one of a vanished harmony with nature. This, in Schiller's diagnosis, had shaped the modes of feeling ('Empfindungs-weisen') of modern European literature, and deep down all its forms aspired to restore the lost harmony. Goethe's *Ganymed* arguably comes closer than any other poem to achieving that. (Its nearest competitor might be some of the near-ecstatic responses to nature in Goethe's novel *Die Leiden des jungen Werthers*, especially the letter of 10 May in Book 1; though Werther's feelings, for nature as well as Lotte, are ultimately frustrated, and his end is tragic.)

So does *Ganymed* with its ecstasies balance and cancel out *Prometheus* with its rebellion? Measuring which of these powerful poems outweighs the other would be a difficult business. Poems are not designed for competition. Would it be helpful to know which of them came second, indicating a change of mind? Interesting, perhaps, but not decisive. Poems cannot be taken as stages in a consistent intellectual development; they express moods and attitudes that may not change in a linear way. Even if they did express successive intellectual positions, would Ganymed's loving impulse flatly reverse Prometheus' defiance and denial? Might it not perhaps even be a new positive beginning that is only possible once the ground has been cleared of old theological concepts of power and authority? As it were, a secularised version of the shift from Old to New Testament...?

An Merck   1774   **(p. 15)**

Goethe sent these verses with a portfolio of his drawings to his friend Johann Heinrich Merck. Goethe was a keen amateur artist, and for a long time had hopes and ambition to be more than that, till the intensive study and practice of art during his two years in Italy (see Notes to *Römische Elegien*, p. 81) convinced him that he had no more than a 'Talentchen'. Drawing, however, still had the value for him of making him look closely at the world of objects, as in a different way his scientific interests did (though his science was in an altogether different class from his art). To speak of 'looking' understates the case, as the core passage of these verses shows. These lines (11-16) are a programme for a comprehensive loving realism.

The manner is appropriate for communication to a friend (Goethe never published the poem), but it is also typical of Goethe's poetry to begin casually and quickly rise to a major theme – even then without necessarily raising the stylistic register, and certainly without becoming solemn. (Cf. below on *Parabase*.)

How seriously the central lines here are meant is suggested by echoes of a key speech from one of the early scenes of *Faust* (perhaps they are pre-echoes – the scene cannot be exactly dated) in which the elderly professor, frustrated with conventional knowledge, turns to magic for deeper insight into reality:

> daß ich erkenne, was die Welt
> Im Innersten zusammenhält   (lines 382f)

What Goethe sends Merck is meant as a recipe for becoming a good artist, but it obviously has a broader human value and would be an achievement in itself.

line 4: 'Zeichen Schal', presumably metaphorical, not literal: the gift of his drawings as a shaped vessel for his friend to take pleasure in and (see next line) draw strength from.

line 5: 'zu feste*m* Kraft und Grund', free-and-easy adjective agreement attracted by the second noun in the phrase.

line 7: 'Nimm's', and *line 8*: 'wenn's um dich schwebt', the 'es' = 'das Pfand' of line 1.

An Schwager Kronos   1774   (p. 15)

Myth again, but again in a different sense. This time there is no originating story; the poem's roots are in the everyday experience of a coach ride, which it raises to general significance. Well, perhaps not quite everyday. Goethe had been escorting Klopstock part of the way home, and Klopstock was *the* poet of the day, hence a name to conjure with. In Goethe's tragic novel *Die Leiden des jungen Werthers* of 1774, Werther and Lotte discover they are soulmates during a storm, which they both experience as a re-run of the storm sublimely described in Klopstock's *Frühlingsfeier*, one of his most famous free-verse poems. The time spent in Klopstock's company may have heightened Goethe's mood during the journey back. (For another instance of the Klopstock effect, see p. 66, on *Auf dem See*.)

'Schwager' was student slang for a coachman; 'Kronos' was the supreme Greek god of a time before Zeus; but here, in a confusion common in Goethe's day, he is taken to be the god of time itself (properly Chronos). For this is time-travel, not just a journey on one day. It does however have all the feel of a real journey – as might be expected of something written in a coach – with the passenger chafing at the slow progress, then enjoying the grand view from the hill-top, stopping for welcome refreshment, and finally anticipating journey's end and a warm reception. The verse, perhaps consciously emulating Klopstock, is 'free', but only in the sense of having no regular metre; otherwise, it is shaped by the changing rhythms of a coach-ride, careering downhill (st. 1), dragging uphill (st. 2), and bumping over a rough eighteenth-century road. This last is captured in l. 7 by not integrating the names of objects into the sentence structure but simply putting them in its way, much as the objects themselves are obstacles in the way of the coach's wheels. Doing violence to normal syntax in the cause of making expression as direct as possible is part of the young Goethe's breakout from convention.

An exhilarating eighteenth-century ride, yet the end foreseen is in Orcus, the underworld of the ancients, the afterlife. But at least it is a triumphant arrival, a prince is greeted by the Mighty Ones, who are presumably famous figures of the past. And he has got there fast enough – line 1 demanded more speed – not to have suffered the long decline and decay of old age. (Here the metaphor of the coach-ride does not exactly match the intended message: time-travel escapes some of the limitations of spatial travel, and need not even mean traversing exactly the same ground.)

Still, the familiar metaphor of life as a journey has been translated into lively detail; or rather, and the difference is crucial, the experience of an actual journey has enlivened the old metaphor and become the personal myth of a vigorous modern speaker who has a high opinion of himself. This is the kind of utterance Goethe may have had in mind when, looking back, he spoke of the 'göttliche Frechheit' of his youthful works (to F.H. Jacobi, 11 January 1808).

line 1: 'Spude', dialect for 'spute'.

line 5: 'Haudern', the dawdling typical of hired drivers, presumably because they are paid by time not distance.

line 10: 'eratmend', 'getting their breath' (viz., the horses).

line 17: 'Über', not here a preposition relating to the noun that follows, but – another minor violence to conventional language – an adverb (= 'high above this mountain scene').

Variants: In the 1789 version, Goethe toned his 'divine impudence' down. The last three lines read:

> Daß der Orkus vernehme: wir kommen,
> Daß gleich an der Türe
> Der Wirt uns freundlich empfange.

He also changed ll. 6f to read:

> Frisch, holpert es gleich, [= obgleich es holpert]
> Über Stock und Steine den Trott...

How do these variants compare with the first version in detail, and how do the changes affect the poem overall?

Neue Liebe, neues Leben 1775 (p. 16)

A playful poem, but not in the Rococo mode. The reluctant lover was not a stock Rococo figure: eager desire was too much the routine motif. But permanent attachment was rarely an issue, so nor was the male wish to avoid it (which was not unknown – it can be found in contemporary drama, e.g. Mellefont in Lessing's *Miss Sara Sampson*).

Or is there something serious beneath the playfulness? Puzzlement at how he ever got drawn in so deep is a constant in the poems inspired by Lili Schönemann, to whom Goethe became (but did not stay) engaged.

An Belinden 1775 (p. 17)

The lovers' different social spheres create tension. The outsider (stylised into the proverbial poet in a garret) who has dreamt of happiness (the 'goldnen Stunden' of st. 3) is now under pressure to join a glittering but alien society summed up in the 'lights and faces' of st. 4. (That motif will be used again for the conventional society of the Weimar court: see *Gehab dich wohl...* p. 20). The psychological pressure is also on him, once drawn into this world, to persuade himself that he can accept it for the sake of their love. The poem works to resolve the tension by declaring that, for all the artificial setting, she is as charming as the natural world beyond 'society', indeed that wherever she is *is* nature. It is a large and potentially unstable concession.

15. Junius 1775, aufm Zürichersee/ Auf dem See (pp. 18 & 19)

Theme and motifs from *An Belinden* are carried over into this poem. After the concession on which the earlier poem ended – wherever she is, is nature – this one has a real natural setting. But pleasure in the scene around him is interrupted by dreams of a past golden time: the tension has not been resolved. To say this is not to reduce the poem to biographical fact, but to read the sequence of poems as a continuous inner history. That is not the same as assuming that they make a consistent linear development. On the contrary, there may be oscillation, vacillation, relapse. On this basis, it is legitimate to ask what kind of resolution this poem reaches for the already familiar dilemma.

The poem does not of course have to be read even with that much context and connection. It is one of the most self-sufficient of lyrics, even in the first, the 'diary' version. That already gives us full grasp of a situation and the sense of a resolution. It does so by evoking a zestful mood in the present, then harking back to a different happiness promised in the past, and finally coming back to the present again. The poetic statement has become not impersonal, but supra-personal; a particular experience has been generalised. Deleting place and date is an obvious part of this process, as is the adding of a generalised title: this could be anyone's emotional quandary, on any lake; its lineaments are real but also archetypal. Goethe later saw and said that 'generalisation' in this subtle sense (*not*, that is, in the sense of 'abstraction') was the direction poetry should move in, though he still insisted that a real occasion ('Gelegenheit') was needed to set it going. (See Introduction, p. xiii.) Otherwise a poem would be a more or less arbitrary construct of the imagination, with that much less authenticity and authority.

It is worth following the whole process through from personal beginnings to finished poem. Lake Zurich, besides its surrounding scenery and views of distant mountains, had a poetic aura because Klopstock had written a celebrated ode there, *Der Zürcher See*. As if that was not enough to bring on the creative mood, Goethe's party played a rhyme-game when they – presumably – got tired of looking about them at the scenery. They passed Goethe's notebook round for the purpose, and it is preserved; on the same page as the last improvised rhymes, separated off from them by two short parallel pencil-strokes in the margin, is Goethe's poem. So although the text has no crossings-out or alterations and looks like a fair copy, it is hard to see how it can be one. The preserved MS seems to be the draft written either in the boat – that is implied by the informal heading, which is not yet consciously a poem-title, and therefore the more to be trusted – or soon afterwards. Goethe often wrote with this on-the-spot promptness, in circumstances that can be reconstructed (cf. *An Schwager Kronos*, *Holde Lili*, and *Elegie*).

There are two further pencil-strokes in the margin after the first eight lines of verse, separating these from the remaining twelve. This suggests that the two sections were originally distinct poems, perhaps the products of two moments (and moods) that closely succeeded one the other. If so, what is the effect of linking them as one poem? And then of dividing the twelve-line section into four-plus-eight, as Goethe did for the first published version of 1789? Whichever way it is laid out on the page, the poetic substance from the first had marked shifts of attitude and emotion, and an extraordinary variety of metre and rhythmic movement that responds to those shifts. (Very roughly, as a start: the first eight lines are iambic, alternating four and three feet; the next four are trochaic, two with four, then two with three-and-a-half feet – and l. 12 begins with that rare thing, a pure spondee; while the last eight lines wonderfully defy summary with their free mix of trochees, anapaests and dactyls.) All these things are worth plotting precisely, as is the subtle shift away from overtly personal expression (ll. 1-12) to what looks at first sight like impersonal description (ll. 13-20). Does this shift break the poem's unity? If not, how does the closing section relate to what has gone before?

There are changes in wording too, most obviously the removal of the stark umbilical cord image with which version 1 opened – a bit too strong, Goethe may have thought, for readers, especially women readers, in his day. But the image has psychological implications beyond its shock effect. The psycho-analyst Otto Rank argued that the birth trauma rather than Freud's Oedipus complex was the prime source of neurosis, and reported that his patients often dreamt themselves back into the womb. Successful analysis was then experienced as a happier rebirth (*Das Trauma der Geburt und seine Bedeutung für die Psychoanalyse*, 1923). The first version of *Auf dem See* enacts something like these processes – with the difference that to heal his love-trauma Goethe appropriates nature on the grand scale as his comforting womb, the very opposite of a neurotic regression, and by l. 3 has duly been reborn. Does this mean the poet can heal his own traumas through the unconscious psycho-analysis of poetry? (The theme will recur in *Trilogie der Leidenschaft*.)

In the final version, the loss of that strong opening image is made up for by the deceptively simple eloquence of the opening word 'Und'. It suggests the speaker is renewing contact with a nature that can always be relied on to be there, waiting to refresh and restore him. It has been more prosaically argued that the 'Und' is only there to pick up from the ending of a preceding poem, and that Goethe never begins a poem with 'Und' unless this is the case (see Eibl 1, 1006 and 2, 1347). This is an unsatisfactory argument because it is potentially circular: if we accept it as a 'rule', this case cannot disprove it. As it happens, the poem which *Auf dem See* followed in the 1789 *Schriften* was *Lilis Park*, another (humorous) sketch of the same uneasy love-relationship: the 'Und' was making successive poems into a connected history even more directly than suggested above. Even that need not be a final reading: as Goethe's poems underwent rearrangement in later editions and *Auf dem See* became detached from its forerunner, the 'Und' acquired an independent force and a greater resonance – which is precisely (though this time accidentally) the process of moving from a specific occasion to a general sense that Goethe aimed at.

Im Herbst   1775   [Revised as **Herbstgefühl** 1789]   **(p. 19)**

Goethe's poetic openings are always direct, but this one is truly extraordinary. Nothing could more instantly evoke rich, succulent growth than the two words 'Fetter grüne', or create a more instant feeling of intimacy with nature than the next two, 'du Laub' – which is nothing like the arm's-length formality of the conventional opening to an ode: 'O...'. And how many nature poems begin with an imperative? It is hardly, though, a real command: leaves are unlikely to grow greener and more succulent on request, in autumn of all times; and it certainly does not signal an impulse to dominate nature. On the contrary, the speaker is rapturously seconding nature in what she is already doing, he is welcoming the process that is happening in front of his eyes, asking for more of the same. It is a highly economical way of simultaneously evoking (it cannot be called describing) the way things are, and expressing pleasure in it: an imperative of delighted assent. It also incidentally avoids the lyrical poet's need to say 'I', while still leaving the personal standpoint absolutely clear. The opening pair of imperative-plus-adverb ('Fetter grüne') is followed by other similar pairs: 'Gedrängter quillet' and 'reifet schneller und glänzend voller' (a first draft had yet another 'und glän*zet* voller'). All this is an exercise in the 'loving realism' for which *An Merck* sketched a programme.

Yet the poem, for all its zest and delight, actually ends on the theme of unhappy love. Running through the several influences that make the grapes grow, the speaker arrives at the fanciful notion that the tears from his eyes (he is leaning out of his window over the climbing vine) are equally necessary, to water them. This might be the old Rococo playfulness again, were it not for the final suggestion that love is a single great force (cf. *Maifest*, p. 53) inherent in the growth of natural things, and that his individual experience is merely one more channel for it. This provides a positive culmination for the finely organised single sentence that starts at l. 7 and makes up the whole second half of the poem, with a repeated 'Euch' (he is still addressing the grapes!) as the constant object of successive verbs: 'Euch brütet', 'euch umsäuselt, 'Euch kühlet' and 'euch betauen'. The climactic 'Ach!' that ends the sequence ought also to mark a turn towards misery. Yet the climax contrives still to sound exhilarating: the lover's individual melancholy has made him aware of the great system he is part of. This is probably the happiest unhappy love poem there is.

line 8: 'Scheideblick' is the sun's parting (autumnal) glance, a look back; but it just might hint at the chemical processes in the grape which the sun is bringing to full ripeness.

Comparisons: the young Bertolt Brecht's nature-poems *Vom Klettern in Bäumen* and *Vom Schwimmen in Seen*, which likewise avoid saying 'I' by a neat use of imperatives, albeit not addressed to nature.

Two letter poems
Holde Lili... and Gehab dich wohl...   1775   (p. 20)

These two poems are linked by their common origin. They were composed on the same day and written down in the same letter to Carl August on 23 December 1775. Goethe probably thought them too simple to publish, if indeed he remembered writing them at all. They were not printed until his correspondence with the Duke was published in 1915.

They might therefore be thought of as primarily biographical documents, and they certainly plot an area of Goethe's Weimar emotional life with the coordinates of a past love and a present friendship. But are they really too simple to be worth attention as poems (and would outward simplicity be an objection anyway)?

The circumstances of their composition make them a fascinating further instance of poetry generating more poetry (cf. note on *Auf dem See* p. 66). Goethe had ridden out with some friends and was putting up in a forester's dwelling. He wrote to Carl August in the evening, appending the first poem, which had come into his mind towards the end of the day's ride. The poetic mood and the act of saying goodnight led him on to write another one. The fact that Goethe never lifted either poem from the soil they grew in is a good reason for presenting them in the full original context.

Wandrers Nachtlied   1776 [Revised 1789]   (p. 20)

This is a prayer, at first sight an orthodox Christian one. Its opening line echoes the Lord's Prayer, and for years it figured in the hymn-book of the Protestant congregation of Bremen. The impression of orthodoxy easily arises because we are not told till near the close who the Being addressed is – not God, but Peace. The long sentence that gives the poem its structure withholds that information by starting with complex relative clauses, delaying further with two interjected questions, and only then providing the answer. That builds up expectation and gives a feeling of relief that matches the supplicant's need. By then the familiar atmosphere of devotion has long taken effect and persuaded the inattentive reader that this is a Christian prayer.

Peace is of course itself a Christian concept (cf. John 14: 27, 'Peace I leave with you, my peace I give unto you'; and Philippians 4: 7, 'the peace of God which passeth all understanding'). But peace is not represented in the poem as a divine gift; it is an independent entity which will come (or not) on direct request. This is not to say Christianity has no role. Goethe consciously draws on it – it is a vital part of literary tradition, i.e., of the resources available to poets. Even atheist writers like Brecht can use religious motifs and a biblical style for their own purposes. The writer's purpose may actually be religious in the broadest sense. Meditation and self-questioning about one's inner life and relation to the shaping forces of existence – spirituality, in short – do not end when orthodox faith ends. This continuity is as much what is meant by 'secularisation' as is any rejection of orthodox faith. It may take the form of borrowing the expressive means of that faith for private ends.

The poem was originally a wholly private utterance, dated 'Am Hang des Ettersberg d. 12. Feb. 76', and sent in a letter to Charlotte von Stein. Goethe revised it for the 1789 edition. The revisions are intriguing. His reasons can once again be guessed. It must have seemed puzzling that anyone should want relief not just from pain but from joy as well (l. 2). The new version, '*Leid* und Schmerzen', made more obvious sense – but perhaps too obvious, because the two things are virtually the same. The puzzle was not resolved but replaced, and with a conventional sentiment.

The trouble is, the new version now made less good sense of what follows than did the original line – whatever its mysterious meaning was. For if someone is 'doubly miserable', there needs to be a double cause. Joy and pain, in some strange way, plainly were that double cause. What strange way could that be? There is a clue in a letter Goethe wrote to Frau von Stein later in the year (16 September 1776): 'Ich bin in einem unendlich reinen Mittelzustand ohne Freud und Schmerz, zusammengepackt von Tausenderlei Umständen ohne gedrängt zu sein'. He welcomes a 'middle state' free from all emotional hassle. So was even positive emotion in its way stressful? That might depend on the force of your feelings, and on how sensitive you were. A second clue is a poem sent to Auguste von Stolberg on 17 July 1777:

> Alles gaben Götter die unendlichen
> Ihren Lieblingen ganz

Alle Freuden die unendlichen
Alle Schmerzen die unendlichen ganz.

That Goethe too felt himself to be a favourite of the gods completes an equation.

Ein gleiches [Wandrers Nachtlied 2]   1780   (p. 21)

Probably the most famous lyrical poem in the German language, partly for the manner of its composition – Goethe wrote it on the wall of a hill-top hut (the 'Ausgabe letzter Wand', in Peter Johnson's enviable pun) – but partly also for its deceptively simple beauty. It is a classic example of how the process of 'freely' following a train of thought and feeling can arrive at a controlled beauty of form, as measured by inner coherence and correspondences and the way minute variations of rhythm ('metre' is too formal a notion for this poem) can capture a distinctive moment and its mood.

The rhythmic movement in the poem is shaped by the tiniest details, above all by four variations on the single letter 'e'. It is left off the end of 'Ruh[e]' but added in or on to the words 'spür*e*st', 'Vög*e*lein' and 'Wald*e*'. These are true sound-effects, variations the poet has chosen or chanced upon in his contemplative frame of mind, and they help him express it to perfection. Try reversing any of them and observe the difference.

This is a quite different finding from the suggestion sometimes made that a particular sound is tied to a whole category of meaning ('p has an inherently sharp, b a blunt effect' – on which see the blunt and sharp remarks in Johnson *GLL*, p. 37). Apart from onomatopeia, i.e., words that originated in the direct imitation of a sound ('hiss', 'boom', 'click'), what has usually happened in such readings is that the critic has taken in the sense and then imagined that the sound made an independent contribution to it. The long vowel in 'Ruh' certainly helps in this poem, but it is less obviously a creative choice on the poet's part – 'Ruhe' simply is the word for 'rest', and the long middle vowel would be just as restful in any context. At most the sound of 'Ruhe' has been preferred to the possible alternative 'Friede' (which the first Wandrers Nachtlied addressed). But the final vowel is another matter: from 'Ruhe' to 'Ruh' in this line is the movement from prose to poetry.

Sound subtly interacts with sense and with the layout of the lines. Where objects have a line to themselves without a verb, as in ll. 1 and 3, it gives them a static feel. (Contrast the effect of openings with a verb – 'Wie herrlich leuchtet', 'Mir schlug das Herz', 'Fetter grüne du Laub'.) When the verbs in this poem do come, the line-break has slowed the pace – it would have been perceptibly different if the first four lines had been laid out as two longer lines; and the sense of these verbs – 'ist', 'spürest' – is not active enough to disturb a scene that is not just quiet but motionless. 'Ruh' means both: an evening stillness. There is a more strongly rhythmic movement to l. 6, but it is a rocking movement; we are not going anywhere except to sleep. The dactyl of 'Vögelein' provides the lilt of a lullaby, and lullaby is also suggested by the form of the word, an archaic, folksong diminutive: all in all, an extraordinary piece of creative economy. Yet none of these effects thrusts itself on us; they are as quiet as the poem's subject. The rhyme-scheme is rendered unobtrusive by the varying line-length, but still provides a gentle cohesion. 'Gipfel' and 'Wipfel' seem to have been made for each other – though MS copies made by Goethe's friends begin 'Über allen Gefilden'. (Perhaps for a while he thought the rhyme was risky, too exact, too close to being a jingle.) The cohesion is gently reinforced by the way the last line, 'Ruhest du auch', echoes the 'Ruh' and 'du' of ll. 2 and 4 as well as the 'Hauch' of l. 5: double internal rhyme plus end-rhyme.

It has been ingeniously suggested that there are intellectual, indeed scientific depths in the sequencing of the sights and sounds the poem registers, for it moves from mineral to vegetable to animal to human ('Gipfel', 'Wipfel', 'Vögelein', 'du'). The progression, once it has been pointed out, is a pleasurable plus, but almost certainly an accidental one. The reason for the sequence was probably more immediate, less analytic: the poet's eye moves from far to near, from a horizon of hills seen at some distance, via trees that are near enough to be seen and heard moving in the breeze, if there were one, and thence to things closer still whose silence the ear cannot miss. This is arguably how Goethe the landscape artist, which at this time he keenly was (whereas he was barely yet into science), will have taken in the evening scene.

It is astounding that Goethe did not publish this poem until 1815, and then perhaps only because someone else had unauthorisedly done so. He then gave it the almost dismissive heading (it is hardly a title) 'Ein gleiches' – 'another of the same kind', viz. as the first *Wandrers Nachtlied*. Did he fail to realise its quality? Did it seem too slight to bother with? We have seen enough evidence that he could be insensitive to his own lyrical achievements. It is true that when in old age he found his poem still there on the hut wall, it moved him deeply; he was reading the last line as an intimation of mortality. Since then, that sense has commonly been assumed to be present. How far does the poem support this reading?

Since Goethe placed the two 'Wandrers Nachtlieder' together in 1815, that is where they have stayed. Following his firm hint, critics have suggested that the mood of the one answers the prayer of the other. What can be said for and against such a double reading? (I break the chronological arrangement of the present edition in this case to make it easier to compare and connect the two poems.)

Warum gabst du uns die tiefen Blicke   1776   (p. 21)

Goethe clearly thought this poem too personal to be included in his works. He sent it, untitled, to Charlotte von Stein in a letter of 14 April 1776 and it was only published in 1848 as part of that correspondence. The 'du' the poet addresses is 'Schicksal' (cf. l. 5), not Charlotte, and it affects her jointly with him. It is however a matter of fated insights more than a fated outcome; the future is mentioned (ll. 2 and 25) but not concretely imagined or aspired to. The poem is more concerned with an imagined or remembered past, from which the intense feelings of the present and vague expectations of the future spring. Specifically, these two people are fated to know each other clear-sightedly – unlike the thousands who know neither themselves nor each other (ll. 10, 16ff). The ignorance of the mass is a kind of happiness, and true insight a rather sad superiority, which is why the opening line is a question yet also a complaint: Charlotte and he are unfortunate (l. 15) in having to live without romantic illusions.

The discomfort of the poet's own insight comes from the obscure sense of a happy previous existence, in which they were brother and sister or man and wife; in comparison with that, the present is necessarily painful (l. 48) and all their experience in it is pale and only half alive (ll. 49f). The most powerful part of the poem is the passage evoking all the beneficial effects of that earlier incarnation (ll. 29-44), where the sequence of second-person verbs builds up a strong sense of intimacy. (Colloquially leaving out the 'du' here has an effect very different from the hostile brusqueness it conveys in st. 1 of *Prometheus*.) Some of these phrases are quoted by biographers as if they were Goethe's gratitude for what Charlotte has been to him in the present. As this is the reason why he imagines a past life together, in substance it is not a falsification. Within the poem, however, the passage is unambiguously a flashback to that life.

Note incidentally the way the pronoun shifts from 'mich' (l. 31) to 'ihn' (l. 37) as the poet steadily objectivises and visualises himself in the imagined past. The gap is smaller here than in *Seefahrt* (see p. 75), but the transition is made possible because the intervening lines all use (as German commonly does but English cannot) the definite article, not the possessive adjective, to refer to parts of the speaker's body and his actions – 'Blut', 'Lauf', 'Brust'.

The poem is a striking mixture of intimacy and high formality: the eight-line rhymed stanzas (with one twelve-line section) are moving towards the chosen form of Goethe's grand reflective statements – the prefatory poem to *Faust*, the dedicatory poem to his collected verse (*Zueignung*), the poem *Urworte. Orphisch* – in all of which he uses the even more closely controlled *ottava rima*, whose rhyme-scheme (*ababab cc*) points up arguments or tensions and draws clear conclusions.

Does this poem's short final line, with the motif that fate may torment but cannot change them, provide a culmination? Or is it a tailing away?

line 2: 'ahn*d*ungsvoll', an eighteenth-century form for 'ahnungsvoll'.

line 8: 'wahr' without the full adjective ending ('wahres') is an archaic or poetic form possible only with neuter nouns.

line 12: 'unversehen', unexpected.

line 14: 'unerwarte', an elided form of the past participle 'unerwartete'.

line 27: 'abgelebt', a past participle that usually means 'antiquated', while the verb/noun form ('ab-/Ableben') means 'decease/to pass away'; but the literal sense of its two parts allows the meaning 'lived through in the past', or even 'in a past life'.

lines 35f: 'ruhte...sich wieder auf', an expressive splicing of two ideas, 'sich aufrichten', to get on one's feet again, and 'ruhen', to rest. The effect is pleasantly paradoxical because a passive state is turned into an activity.

Seefahrt   1776   (p. 22)

Another 'destiny' poem, again creating a personal myth, and again using the topos of a journey; not this time from personal experience, but by imaginative projection (Goethe did not even set eyes on the sea until 1786).

This is a kind of anniversary poem looking back on Goethe's situation of a year before, when he had been invited to Weimar but was kept waiting for the expected transport. It was published in the September with the simple title 'Goethe den 11. September 1776', virtually as a public statement to the friends who knew of the move and were interested in him and his fate. In the poem, these become the friends who drink with him while he waits, and who watch in fear and sympathy as his struggle with the elements begins. That does not mean we have to link every motif in the poem to the events of that first year, as Eibl does (1, 931f). An imaginary voyage suggests its own atmosphere and incidents, the nights of great star-filled skies, the brewing storm and its onslaught. Nor does it mean that the 'open' ending, with its high hopes and trust in his gods, is somehow inauthentic because Goethe's own journey had meanwhile turned out for the best. That was not yet wholly beyond dispute: only a much longer time would show whether going to Weimar had been the 'right' decision. Indeed its rightness has sometimes been questioned since.

Yet the new shape Goethe's life had taken was perhaps a factor in the formal control and narrative coherence that sets this poem off from others that are located on the same borderland between personal statement and myth – *Wandrers Sturmlied, Prometheus, Ganymed*. Instead of a verse that freely follows the movements of thought and feeling, as in those poems, there is now an unforced regularity of form: mostly five-foot trochaic lines with only a few variations into a longer or (to mark a stanza ending) a shorter line. The result is a story that unfolds with a leisurely yet purposeful movement exactly matching its themes, from the impatience and uncertainty of delay, through the bustle of departure and the first full breeze in the sails, then the threat and arrival of the storm and the possibility of disaster, to the closing image of a man bravely facing his fate. The form seems to breathe the more disciplined freedom of a voyager's purposeful response to the perilous yet exhilarating elements.

The sense of purpose, peril and response is there at the most basic level in the conjunctions that start the stanzas. First there is the 'Und...Und...Und' of the departure and the pleasures of the voyage: beginning a sentence with 'Und' is a legacy of the Bible's narrative style and suggests a significant, perhaps a divinely intended course leading to an expected fulfilment. Then come the two adversatives, 'Aber...Aber', casting the shadow of the storm; while 'Und' in its other function introduces the consequence of its coming, that his friends fear for him. Finally a 'Doch' overrides those fears and reasserts the hero's power to survive.

Other shifts within the narrative raise questions. At the outset the hero is a merchant taking passage with the ship ('Güterfülle' in l. 7), but at the close he is himself the steersman. Has there been a shift from the desire for profit to a wider adventurousness, brought about through the elemental experience of the storm? Most noticeably the poem begins as first-person narrative ('saß...Ich im Hafen'), but by mid-way (l. 23) the voyager has become a third-person 'er'. Could this be a switch to the standpoint of his watching friends? No such shift is made clear, as it later explicitly is when they are described watching in fear for his safety. The inconsistency is formally hard to resolve, but perhaps not hard to understand. Expressing subjective emotions through the person of the voyager allows the poet to see himself objectively; as he writes, the objectivising process steadily takes over. It can do this the more easily when there is a big gap, as there is here, between the successive references to a personal subject – 'dir' in l. 10 and 'ihn' in l. 23. (Cf. Note on *Warum gabst du uns die tiefen Blicke*, p. 73.)

There are some fine evocative touches, for a poet who had never been on board a ship and would not even see the sea for another decade. He did, though, know his Homer.

line 3: 'erzechend', 'working up courage by carousing', and l. 12: 'entjauchzt', 'rouses us out of sleep with shouts of rejoicing' – two finely economical compressions of sense achieved by the use of German's powerful verbal prefixes.

Eis-Lebens Lied 1776 (p. 24)

Goethe's youthful confidence is not just blithe cockiness, as the touches of self-deflating humour in *Wandrers Sturmlied* show. The present short poem uses the image of skating, on possibly thin ice, to capture the oscillations of morale that underlie ambition and make self-confidence more of a struggle than a permanent state. Motifs follow and question each other within a brief compass. First the emphatic 'sorglos' – but can he really be so carefree when he can see before him expanses that even the boldest skaters have not dared to go onto? Then comes the brave self-exhortation to mark out his own way independently. But this in turn makes his heart thump. Finally, he has to calm it with the reassurance that the ice will not break; or if it does, it will not be when he is on it, an irrational trust in a providence all his own.

The word 'Leben' in the poem's title makes this an allegory of individual destiny akin to *An Schwager Kronos*. Goethe's revised title for the 1789 edition, *Mut*, loses this by not pointing beyond the concrete situation the poem describes. Perhaps Goethe wanted to lose it, so as to avoid seeming to make grander claims.

Erlkönig 1782 (p. 24)

Ballads, like folksong (cf. *Heidenröslein*), were part of the new conception of a natural popular culture of which Herder was the prime champion. For this poem he also provided a model, his translation of a Danish ballad under the title *Erlkönigs Tochter*. The Danish 'ellerkonge' ('elf-king') obscurely suggested a link with 'Erlen' ('alder-trees') and made this mysterious being seem some sort of wood-sprite. Uncertainty about what the word meant can only have added to the effect on German readers. More importantly, Goethe takes over the form without a definite article (cf. p. 52 on *Heidenröslein*). Starkly devoid of the accompanying word, it suggests an uncompromising alien presence.

Real popular ballads, again like folksong, were commonly long and repetitious, although the repetition of a refrain did sometimes have a powerful ominous effect (e.g. in the Scottish border ballad *Edward*). Goethe's ballad, in contrast, is highly economical. Both the narrative stanzas proper (the first and last, which set the scene and tell the ending) and the three-cornered dialogue stanzas in between which lucidly carry the rest of the story, could hardly be more terse. For example, the forms of address – 'Mein Vater', 'mein Sohn', 'Du liebes Kind' – avoid all need to spell out who is speaking to whom, and thus avoid breaking the mounting tension of the spoken exchanges.

Moreover, these exchanges are structured in a way that conveys by itself almost as much as their verbal content. The child's cry of fear and the father's attempt to reassure him are always kept together within the bounds of one and the same stanza. In contrast, Erlkönig's enticements always have a stanza to themselves, they are a self-contained other world to which the father has no access. The first father-son exchange has only one line in which the father tries to explain away the boy's fears; the second has two lines, more reassurance is needed now, a word is repeated for emphasis, though the phrasing is gently varied: 'Sei ruhig, bleibe ruhig'; the third time the father sounds less patient, he repeats 'Mein Sohn, mein Sohn' – at last responding in kind to the child's desperate 'mein Vater, mein Vater' – although the father still insists he is seeing aright ('genau') what he believes the child's phantasies are distorting. But at Erlkönig's third speech, now no longer offering pleasure but threatening force, he has got the child in the same stanza with him; the boy can now only appeal desperately from out of it to the father whose stanza and residually safe mental space he has up to now shared. At the fourth time of asking, the father – tellingly – does not even reply, he has no answers left, he can only ride urgently on, seized by a terror that is now as real as his son's.

But what *is* real in the poem? Traditionally it has been read as a contest between the rational (very roughly, the Enlightenment, which tried to discredit superstition and lighten human darkness) and the irrational (which Romanticism was to reinstate as a real and potentially fruitful force). An age acutely aware of child-molesting has begun to take the poem's detail more literally, much as an age of feminism has done with *Heidenröslein*. Post-Freudian readings hint that the child's sexuality is stirred – though the text speaks only of his terror, and at no point does he seem tempted by Erlkönig's blandishments. Some commentators have even peered suspiciously at Goethe's affection for Charlotte von Stein's son Fritz, though without yet discovering any adequate grounds to do so. In point of outcome, the poem is commonly said to prove the child was right and the father wrong: that is, there are more things in heaven and earth than are dreamt of in the Enlightenment's philosophy. Against that it has been argued that a sick child – is this not perhaps why the father is carrying him so urgently through the night? – may suffer delirious imaginings that keep pace with his worsening state right to the (and his) end. Yet the poem gives no clear sign that the child *is* sick; and without that comforting hypothesis, it seems to be saying that the child has seen and suffered something terribly real. On the other hand, it is not obvious how Erlkönig can have taken physical possession of the 'schöne Gestalt' he loves and desires: the child is simply dead, and this is not a tale about a devil seeking an innocent young soul.

Schubert's famous song-setting captures the urgency of the ride, the mounting terror, and the awful final fact. Loewe's setting subtly conveys Erlkönig's sinister insinuating voice.

Vor Gericht (before 1778) (p. 25)

The poet's intense self-concern need not narrow his human sympathies. A full imaginative awareness of the self may even be a route into the harsh realities that press upon other individuals – real people, that is, not just mythic figures like Faust and Prometheus whom Goethe borrowed as means to explore and express his own feelings and situation. This poem clearly enters into another human being's crisis. It is nevertheless monologue again, with no distancing narrative framework: the most direct form of empathy. The entering-in is complete from the start, the poet speaks not just for the person, but from within the person, as the person.

There is the same concern for the unmarried mother here as in *Faust*, the Gretchen scenes of which were already written before Goethe copied this poem into his manuscript collection in 1778. Gretchen kills her child, is overwhelmed by her guilt, and embraces her death sentence for the sake of her salvation. But this anonymous young woman confronts her accusers with pride and defiance and is assertively loyal to her man, whom she will not identify even by social class (ll. 7f). Perhaps she still expects he will come back and restore her honour in the eyes of the world. In her own eyes, and in God's, it is untarnished (ll. 4 and 12). So what right have they to insult or interrogate her? Meanwhile, the bond to her child is as firm as the bond with her absent lover. Her heart (the poem's theme is the strength of the heart, not the weakness of the flesh) is doubly in the right place.

The poem is social criticism, not abstract and rhetorical, but using the means that are literature's greatest strength: a real situation and a real speaker, a marked character brought alive in idiomatic phrasing and a personal rhythm that fits into a simple, flexibly handled stanza.

Comparisons: Besides Goethe's *Urfaust* or *Faust I*, Schiller's poem *Die Kindsmörderin*; Benjamin Franklin's monologue 'The Speech of Miss Polly Baker', in: Benjamin Franklin, *The Autobiography and other writings* (Penguin Classics 1986).

Grenzen der Menschheit 1780 or 1781 (p. 26)

Between 1779 and 1785, Goethe wrote a number of overtly philosophical poems. However rich his earlier poetry had been in implied positions, he had never used the language of abstract reflection. Here stanzas are meant to construct an argument and are linked by words that point up continuity or contrast – especially conjunctions like 'wenn/dann', 'denn', 'aber' – and lead to a conclusion.

Grenzen der Menschheit can be compared directly with *Prometheus* and *Ganymed*, whose positions it seems to take back – Goethe placed *Grenzen* immediately after those two poems in all his collected editions. Neither defiance of nor union with the gods is any longer at issue; there are clear boundaries between us and them. Does this imply giving up the claims of the outstanding individual in favour of humble subordination?

No such precise new doctrine emerges clearly. If human beings measure themselves against the gods by aspiring too high, they will lose their earthly footing (st. 2). Yet if they stick too firmly to the earth, they will get nowhere much, and be less significant than plants (st. 3). So what *are* they (we!) to do?

Stanza 4 turns to a different though central question and answers it with a new image, and the final stanza switches images again. There is an uneasy sense that the poet is casting around for allegorical parallels rather than responding to a compelling single vision. The images of these two stanzas actually conflict: to be raised and then swallowed by waves on which the gods merely look down is a different matter from being confined in a ring which in some unexplained way helps constitute the gods' endless existence.

What 'ihres' in l. 41 refers to has been much discussed, but it is surely the gods. Taking it to refer to the 'Geschlechter' of l. 39 would only give a banal sense – that the sequence of generations may be thought of as an endless chain, at most a suggestion that mankind in the mass is more significant than in the piece. In that case, though, one would expect a strong adversative – not 'Und' but '*Doch* viele Geschlechter...'. More importantly, that reading would go against the poem's whole rhetoric of contrast between mankind and the gods, and its central argument that we are limited whereas they are eternal. An earlier manuscript version had 'reihen *sie* dauernd', which even more clearly makes 'ihres' refer to the gods' existence.

So why did Goethe exchange a clear for an even slightly ambiguous formulation? (The printed version cannot well be a misprint, since 'sie and 'sich' look too different in eighteenth-century handwriting to be easily mistaken.) Did he perhaps want to reduce the gods' active role? They do not have much of one in the rest of the poem, after the 'segnende Blitze' of st. 1 – and since the places where lightning strikes the earth become for chemical reasons more fertile, even that may be more a metaphor than a literal statement of divine intervention. There is no suggestion that divine punishment threatens human beings if they go against the prohibition set up in st. 2. Where the phrase 'reihen sie' made the gods into agents, 'reihen sich' means that the process happens by itself. That would be consistent with the gods' non-active role. It also fits in well with the idea that successive human rings compose the chain of the gods' existence, which suggests that, despite the 'Grenzen' which the poem set out to expound, the gods are dependent on human beings. For worship, perhaps, as the necessary condition of their existence? That was already the dismissive view of the gods that *Prometheus* took (especially st. 3), though in this later poem it is put in a more conciliatory tone; but it would still mean that the poem, humbler gestures and all, was not so different in its substance.

Das Göttliche   1783 (p. 27)

This poem about 'the divine' – a less concrete, less doctrinally limiting term than 'God' – significantly does not begin with its stated theme, but with exhortations to humans to behave humanely, and thereby show themselves different from all other known beings. That, however, is made to depend (st. 2) on having a conception of unknown higher beings whom we try to imitate. We arrive at 'the divine' from human aspiration.

For the most part, the world is governed by the cold necessities listed in sts. 3 and 4 (including nature which, unusually for Goethe, is here described as unfeeling). All of this, st. 5 sums up as inexorable laws. But the freedom to resist necessity and create a distinctively human world (sts. 7 and 8) leads back finally to that conception of divine beings that first inspired it. The tone towards the end becomes a touch triumphal; there is no longer the original sense of how precarious the humane world is, depending as it does on a standard set only by humanity's own hopeful intuitions.

It has sometimes been objected that you cannot imitate something you only have such a vague idea of. This seems short-sighted. It imposes too low a ceiling on human aspiration and, given the doubtful evidential status of the various religious revelations, it would invalidate most of the world's transcendent beliefs. The poem's logic is a virtuous circle: a hopeful hypothesis about divine beings – i.e., about the ultimate nature of reality – will inspire humane acts. If these prove successful, the hypothesis becomes stronger and inspires more acts of the same kind. And so on. This creative use of provisional belief is an Enlightenment idea found in other writers of the day, e.g. in Kant's theory of history (*Idee zu einer allgemeinen Geschichte in weltbürgerlicher Absicht*, 1784). It is fully worked out in dramatic terms in Goethe's play *Iphigenie auf Tauris*, written at about the same date as this poem (prose version 1779; revised verse text 1787). There too the adjective 'ehern' (l. 32) describes the grim necessities that humane action has to overcome.

The crucial point in the poem's argument is l. 10: 'Ihnen gleiche der Mensch'. Strangely, that line only appears in the MS version and not in any text printed in Goethe's lifetime. Was it left out by mistake, as most later editors have assumed? Or did Goethe cut it because he doubted the logic of the virtuous circle himself? If so, it would be another instance of the poet as critic falling below the level of imaginative coherence and persuasiveness his own poem had achieved.

Mignon 1783? (p. 29)

This is a song sung by Mignon, the strange girl-child who accompanies an equally mysterious wandering harper in the novel *Wilhelm Meisters Lehrjahre*. The only thing in their tragic past that has a bearing on the song is that they have come from Italy. The changing address – 'Geliebter', 'Beschützer', 'Vater' – reflect Mignon's shifting relations in the narrative to Wilhelm, and perhaps to the old Harper. (The earlier version found in Goethe's fragmentary first draft of the novel, *Wilhelm Meisters theatralische Sendung*, has 'Gebieter' in place of all three forms of address.)

Goethe wrote the poem well before his own time in Italy, during which he settled on Vicenza as the town that Mignon must come from. His imagination is thus trying to realise a land that he has not yet seen, but has long yearned to. It does so in strongly evocative visual, almost visionary terms: the intensity of colour in st. 1, and in st. 2 the setting in what could be a villa by the Renaissance architect Andrea Palladio (whom Goethe was later bowled over by) complete with marble statues. The mountain passes on the route over the Alps (st. 3) were scenes Goethe did already know. Yearning to be somewhere else is a frequent motif from the late eighteenth century on into Romanticism. It is rare for yearning to be made quite so concrete; here emotion is almost wholly absorbed in the objects and sights named. That is a foretaste of Goethe's Classical aesthetics.

At first glance it seems the regular stanza will have an equally regular metre. But the opening 'Kennst du...' is a trochee. We go into the poem on a natural speech rhythm different from the iambic lines that will follow. It is typical of Goethe's easy colloquial transition into poetic vision – and, in a sense, out of it again; for the phrase returns as a refrain that brings us back from images of Italy to an almost casual conversational tone ('Kennst du es wohl?') – before the final line and a half of each stanza are suddenly caught up in the urgency of Mignon's appeal.

Römische Elegien 1788 (p. 29)

This cycle of love-poems is one of Goethe's greatest and most warmly human creative acts, and a milestone in more than just his individual writing career. The *Elegies* cast off the inhibition and titillation that made up the common European past and begin to shape a new literary future by evoking a simple Roman present.

In 1786 Goethe escaped from his administrative burdens and an increasingly difficult relationship with Charlotte von Stein and spent nearly two years in Italy, largely in Rome. He studied art and architecture, finished some of the longer works for which his Weimar duties had left him too little time, and felt himself recovering from the psychic oppressiveness of what he called the 'Cimmerian' – irretrievably gloomy – north.

There had been Classical allusions in Goethe's very earliest poems, in line with the Rococo conventions of the day (cf. Note on *An den Schlaf* and *Die Nacht*, pp. 50-1), but the Classical world now ceased to be a cultural authority to be acknowledged and became for him a way of life to be relived. This is neatly put in the paradox the god of love speaks in Elegy XIII, that Antiquity was once new, and could come alive again for a modern man who had the courage of his emotions:

War die Antike doch neu, da jene Glücklichen lebten.
　　Lebe glücklich, und so lebe die Vorzeit in dir!

Not just happiness but a poetry of happiness would result, something relatively rare in European love lyric which has mostly drawn its themes and its emotional power from the various kinds of misery and frustration that love is heir to – separation, rejection, loss, yearning, female mystery, worship from afar, etc. With few exceptions (John Donne in English) poetry was less a celebration of love than an alternative to it, a consolation for unavailable fulfilment. The *Roman Elegies* emphatically break with that tradition and treat sexual happiness seriously and fully. The word 'Elegies' in the title, by the way, does not indicate an 'elegiac' (sad) mood; it is the name of the form Goethe was borrowing from Latin, the 'elegiac couplet', or 'distich', made up of a hexameter plus a pentameter. (On these see the Note on Metre, p. xxvii.) The choice of form had consequences beyond just visibly emulating the Ancients. Goethe said years later to Eckermann (25 February 1824) that if he had written these poems in the tone and verse-form of Byron's *Don Juan*, which treats sex with a cynical wit pointed up by saucy rhymes, the effect would have been despicable ('verrucht').

We do not know whether Goethe had sexual encounters in Rome; there is certainly no evidence of a *love*-affair of the kind the Elegies narrate. But he began one immediately after he returned to Weimar, taking a young woman of no social or cultural pretensions – i.e., the antithesis of Frau von Stein – into his house. (Her name was Christiane Vulpius; he married her years later, in 1806.) At all events, the two experiences, physical love and a historic city, are fused in the semi-fiction of the *Römische Elegien*, originally called 'Erotica Romana'. The adjective, on whichever side it is placed, is as important as the noun, for Rome is not just a neutral backdrop to the poems. Its buildings, history, art and ethos, and the example of the great Latin love poets, all help to shape the affair. The very name 'Roma' is a palindrome of 'Amor', and in Elegy I the new arrival feels love pulsing through the stones of the buildings like a circuit from which only he is excluded. Not for long.

Promptness is part of the Classical point, and by the start of Elegy II love has been not just found but consummated.

So **Elegy III** finds the poet reassuring the lady that this is as it should be: witness the way that ancient gods and goddesses and other figures of legend took their chances. He contrasts in passing the slow poison of a long-drawn-out love, surely a reference to his long and unfulfilled relationship with Charlotte von Stein. But promptness is not just the message, it is also part of the form. The syntax and word-order themselves enact promptness: in l. 8 through the semi-chiasmus of 'Begierde...Blick...Genuß...Begier', and intensively throughout the closing six lines. Three times love generates an instant response, with cause separated from effect (action, procreation) by no more than an 'und', suggesting both speed and unquestionable rightness. The effect is felt with a shiver on the skin in the juxtaposition 'heiß in die nächtliche Flut' (l. 14). To cap all, the last line and a half takes us straight from the she-wolf's suckling of Romulus and Remus to Rome's mastery of the world which was the ultimate result – a complete history of the city and the nation compressed into one simple linking word.

Elegy V also celebrates close linkage, or rather two linkages – of love and the study of Antiquity, and of love and the writing of poetry. Love is at the centre of both the receptive and the creative process. If it robs the lover of study-time but gives him happiness in return, this is not just the fair exchange expressed in the balance of l. 6. It leads on to the question – a purely rhetorical one! – whether the lover of a living body is not also studying, learning to appreciate marble forms when he makes love, and vice versa; and from there it leads on to the elegant answer given in l. 10. This is a play of reversals that is more complex than a normal chiasmus, yet still totally lucid. The line divides the activity of eye from that of hand, but the two half-lines also complement each other; they break down the division by mingling both activities. Eye has learnt to feel, hand has learnt to see, which makes a kind of chiasmus. But each half-line has not two but three elements, and the words for seeing and feeling and the organs of sight and touch alternate through the line *ababab*. They thus bridge the caesura that at first sight divides the two activities: *aba/bab*. This further emphasises the point, that the enhancement of one pleasure by another or of one sense by another is stronger than any difference and division. Few lines of poetry manage to embody their meaning so perfectly in their form.

The writing of poetry, however, is clearly subordinate to loving, so this is not a linkage between equals. There may be a faint echo here of the old assumption that love-making and love-lyric excluded each other, you *either* did the one *or* wrote the other. Here in contrast poetry both follows, and follows from, love-making. With (unusually?) the woman now asleep and the man still awake, he is free to make up lines of verse and to muse on his predecessors, the Latin poets whose way of love and literature he is consciously reliving; though Kommerell nicely pointed out (p. 231) that Propertius' mistress Cynthia would not have much liked being made a metrical makeshift.

Elegy IX rescues the old metaphor of love as fire (flame, ardour etc.) and gives it fresh life. It describes a lovers' night together by following the fortunes of a real fire in the room. Not however by a nudge-wink refusal to speak directly. The phases of the fire imply very plainly the acts of love for which it is providing light and warmth. Yet the two things, fire and love, are kept separate, each in its literal meaning; the fire is never mere metaphor, it is a real part of the scene and the story. That means it decidedly is a symbol, i.e., a reality that powerfully suggests another reality, but without losing its independent existence. The two realities come together to make an explicit metaphor only in the last line's last words, where both fire and love are dormant, in their morning-after 'ashes' phase; though not for long.

Klein ist unter den Fürsten... 1789 (p. 31)

This poem ended up among the *Venezianische Epigramme* published in 1800, although written before the 1790 journey that gave rise to them. It fits the mood of that sequence, which is mostly grumpy and disillusioned with Italy, for it starts by reproaching the world at large, especially Europe and Germany, for giving the poet so little support and reward. That is then largely a foil to his warm appreciation of Carl August as friend and employer. There is also a tribute to the Duke's role as a public figure (ll. 3 to 6, added to an earlier version that Goethe never published): in the 1780s, Carl August had been politically active trying to unify the smaller German principalities into a 'Third Germany' that it was hoped would balance the power of the two big rival states, Austria and Prussia, and at least be independent of them.

The words of l. 3, 'So wende nach innen...die Kräfte', can also be read as gratitude for literary patronage, which was not what Carl August originally had in mind when he brought Goethe to Weimar – he wanted an intelligent and energetic administrator. Goethe nevertheless became court poet too. Enlightened literary patronage was a rare thing in Germany at the time: a plethora of princes, including as pre-eminent a national figure as Frederick the Great, failed to encourage German artists, preferring more prestigious foreign (especially French) cultural products. And patronage was still a much-needed factor in artistic careers, in the absence of a fully developed market. For example, there was no such thing as book or stage copyright to help guarantee a writer's income.

Did the opening words 'Klein ist...' not risk giving offence? No ruler wants to be called 'small', and court poets usually exaggerate the prince's greatness. But Goethe was not just a court poet, and Carl August was too much his friend to need abject flattery. In any case, the poem's ending more than balances its opening. It elevates the Duke above any contemporary German or even European potentate, and sets him on the level of the Roman Emperor Augustus and his contemporary Maecenas, who was such a famous friend and supporter of writers (Virgil, Horace, Propertius) that his name gave German its word for a patron ('Mäzen').

Metamorphose der Tiere   1798?   (p. 31)

From the 1780s on, Goethe was a passionate scientific observer and experimenter, and wrote extensively on anatomy, botany, geology and optics. He also tried to integrate his scientific ideas into his overall poetic vision, not least by writing poems on technical scientific themes. This was a further tradition he took over from Antiquity: the large-scale poem on the universe that he planned from the mid-1780s was a plain emulation of Lucretius' *De rerum natura* (*On the way things are*). Though not published until 1820, *Metamorphose der Tiere* is almost certainly a fragment from that project. It uses Lucretius' form, the hexameter; and its opening line clearly places it as a part – perhaps as the climax – of a larger argument.

In substance Goethe's account of animal development is pre- and to some extent proto-evolutionary. Like other philosophers and scientists of his day, he rejected teleology, the doctrine that creatures and their individual organs were designed to fulfil purposes, all of these in turn serving the Creator's overall purpose. Instead Goethe argued that natural beings and their forms were self-sufficient. But without a mechanism such as Darwin was later to propose, of random genetic variations that made creatures better able, or less able, to survive and propagate their like – 'natural selection' (*On the Origin of Species*, 1859) – it was not clear how those self-sufficient forms had got there. Goethe speculated that they developed by the transformation ('metamorphosis') of a small number of basic forms – as Darwin was to do at the close of his book. Goethe also saw that creatures' forms must interact with their mode of life, so he was getting close to the notion of environmental pressure that became even more crucial in Darwin's theory of natural selection. But Goethe clung, as Darwin's open-ended thinking did not, to the idea of a controlling order and harmony. His references to nature as a mother, and to creatures as her children, each with its own 'Bestimmung' (ll. 3f, 11, 22), smuggle something very like divine intention in again by the back door.

As the basis of the natural order, Goethe imagines that each creature has a ration of 'metamorphic' energy contained in a circle or within borders (ll. 30f). If it develops one major useful organ, it will not develop another.

Any tendency to such excess would be self-destructive, and not least would destroy the beauty of form: Goethes conception of the natural order has a strong aesthetic element (cf. l. 39, and especially the culminating vision in ll. 50ff). That links poetic with scientific thinking. It is the Muse (l. 60) who vouchsafes these scientific insights. The poem is not just packaging for a theory; it takes poetic imagination to conceive the workings of a harmonious order. We need not accept Goethes ideas fully and literally in order to appreciate his generous vision, which attempts to integrate ethics and even politics with natural forces (ll. 54ff).

Sonette c.1800 (published 1806 and 1802) (p. 33)

Goethe was not a natural sonneteer. He wrote no sonnets before middle age, and even then only one substantial set – seventeen poems (1807-8) that rather cryptically chronicle the phases and episodes of a love-affair – plus the present linked pair. These are both, so to speak, meta-sonnets; that is, they reflect on the sonnet form in much the same way as Wordsworth does in the sonnet 'Nuns fret not at their convent's narrow room'. The first of them treats the constrictions of the form critically, the second records Goethe's rapprochement with it, slightly grudging and noticeably no longer confronting the form's concrete problems, but put as a very general acceptance of control, concentration and law as necessary conditions of high artistic achievement. This second sonnet, especially its final line, has accordingly been a long-standing favourite for quotation because of its clear message. Yet the message is called in question by so much of Goethe's own greatest writing, which is not at all subject to any prior 'law', that this pro-sonnet sonnet could be seen as an example of the too easy drawing of conclusions to which the sonnet form lends itself. Goethe's anti-sonnet sonnet, on the other hand, states more concretely the difficulties that a poet without formalistic inclinations may experience when pressed to use a highly artificial form.

This, at the turn of the century, was a specific pressure of cultural politics. The sonnet in its Petrarchan form was preached and practised by the German Romantics, part of whose chosen mission was to take up the forms and content of the medieval and Renaissance literatures of Christian Europe, especially the Romance literatures of Catholic Spain and Italy, and to establish them in Germany against the Classical tradition. Writing or not writing sonnets became virtually a signal of commitment to the Romantic programme, of which Goethe and even more his friend and ally Schiller disapproved, not least for its religious attachments (perhaps glanced at in the 'heil'ge Pflicht' of the second line of Sonnet 1). The young Goethe had been in substance a pioneer of European Romanticism, but he was chary of this younger generation of self-styled Romantics, their airy programme, exotic tastes and formal laxity – to which the sonnet was something of an exception. So when using this form of 'theirs', he draws a moral of Classical order from it.

The first quatrain of **Sonnet 1** imagines contemporary partisans speaking, and probably the second quatrain does too. True, this one could at a pinch be the poet himself trying to see their point of view. The first tercet, beginning 'So möcht' ich' (l. 9), would then be his statement of intent to do what they want. More likely, though, the line is still reporting their exhortations: 'So [they say] I should...'. That is confirmed by the subjunctive, 'gäbe', in l. 11. The final tercet would then be (as the 'Nur' strongly suggests) his response: reasons for *not* agreeing to do what they want, put in the telling metaphor of carving wood in the piece, which makes him reluctant to work by gluing bits together.

Sonnet 2 has no such dialogic complexities, but is the poet's voice throughout. It directly states his change of mind, albeit with traces of foot-dragging in ll. 3 and 5, and perhaps also in the cautious 'scheinen' of l. 4. The second quatrain puts the case for first learning your trade thoroughly, after which feeling will be free once again to 'glühen' – a word that echoes Goethe's earliest poems (*Prometheus*, *Wandrers Sturmlied*). The tercets then generalise with what begins to feel like a somewhat heavy hand; and the words 'Bildung' and 'Meister' remind us we are listening to the author of the recent 'Bildungsroman' *Wilhelm Meisters Lehrjahre* (1796), in whose later sections individual impulse is a touch too strongly reined back in the cause of socialisation.

In the course of the controversies just sketched, Goethe's sonnet-critical sonnet came to be too much quoted for his liking, and he regretted having seemed to attack a poetic form as such; for the important thing in principle was surely what a poet put into the form (letter to Zelter of 22 June 1808). It does not follow that Goethe had been wrong in practice about his own case, and about the drawbacks of the sonnet for his own kind of creativity.

Dauer im Wechsel 1803 (p. 34)

Few poems combine such a clear line of argument with such evocative images of the pleasures and losses of life. Was it generated by abstract reflection that then drew on real memories? Or did a moment of lyrical feeling expand into cogent thought? It certainly starts from a specific moment that brings home transience poignantly to the observer. In fact, it exaggerates the brevity of blossom, which lasts longer than 'nur Eine Stunde'. From that starting-point it reviews the other seasons (sts. 1 and 2) in search of something in the flux that lasts, only to find that every phase dies into the next – blossoms into leaves into fruit into the seed that starts a new cycle.

The argument culminates in the aphorism, echoing the Greek pre-Socratic philosopher Heraclitus, that you never swim twice in the same river – i.e., the place may be the same, but it is always different water, time changes even the most seemingly constant things. The poem then goes beyond that perception, or rather looks back reflexively at the swimmer himself: for by the same token it is never the same you that swims in the river, or does anything for a second time. The beholder's eye that sees, the lover's lip that kisses, the mountaineer's foot that climbs with the impudent agility of a chamois ('Gemsenfreche', l. 24), the sociable hand that helps, the whole structure of the human form ('das gegliederte Gebilde', l. 27) – they have all been replaced by new growth of tissue in the wave-flow of time. ('An jener Stelle', incidentally, more probably means not 'in that place' – what single place could here be meant? – but 'in place of [all] those', 'an Stelle jener', i.e., 'jener' is the genitive plural of the pronoun, not the dative singular of the adjective. Cf. Goethe's drama *Iphigenie auf Tauris*, l. 744: 'Auf jener Wille lauschen' – 'to listen to the will of those [gods]'.)

All this sounds like a lead-in to the poetic motif that we should make the most of life while we can, familiar from Horace's Latin formula 'carpe diem' (*Odes* I, xi) down to Herrick's 'Gather ye rosebuds while ye may' and beyond; or, with an opposite and Christian emphasis, that we should turn away from the world, however beautiful it may be, and look to the soul's welfare – e.g. Gerard Manley Hopkins's 'That Nature is a Heraclitean Fire, and of the comfort of the Resurrection'. Goethe, typically, conforms to neither. His final stanza simply affirms change and says, in the first instance to himself: let it happen, let beginning and end join in a circle, accept that you are even more transient than the objects you see changing all the time all round you. In other words, accept that you are part of the natural order. Yet the tone is one of positive commitment, strangely almost of exhilaration. That is part of the comfort Goethe offers, as well as the explicit message that we will have been the bearers and utterers of human thought and feeling, and that the forms we generate may last. To that extent, the poem has ended by finding something permanent in flux.

But is this a comfort for poets only?

Comparison: the concluding sonnet of Wordsworth's *River Duddon* cycle of 1820 ('I thought of thee...'), with the lines:

> I see what was, and is, and will abide:
> Still glides the Stream, and shall for ever glide;
> The form remains, the Function never dies; [...]

And: Enough, if something from our hands have power
To live, and act, and serve the future hour.

West-östlicher Divan   (1819)

In 1814 Goethe began writing lyrics in the Persian style, inspired by transla-
tions which Josef von Hammer-Purgstall had published in 1812 of the poet
Hafiz (*d.* 1389). The result was not just one, but a whole series of cycles which
together made up a substantial volume under the title *West-östlicher Divan*.
Poems went on being added, and were published in an expanded *Divan* in
the 'Ausgabe letzter Hand' in 1827. 'Divan' is the Persian for 'collection',
and 'west-östlich' points up the even balance of the two cultures, the sym-
pathetic adoption of eastern modes and motifs by a western poet.

Goethe immersed himself in Persian poetry, thought and history – so
effectively in fact that he was able to write a substantial appendix of essays
filled with detailed knowledge to help the reader understand the foreign culture
(*Noten und Abhandlungen zum besseren Verständnis des West-östlichen
Divans*). All this does not make the poems mere pastiche or illustrations of
exotic knowledge. Helped by some striking parallels between his and Hafiz'
times, Goethe uses the foreign forms and materials to convey the accumulated
experience and personal vision of his own seventh decade. In the public
sphere, they were both poets at a court, and Goethe had just lived through the
upheavals of the Napoleonic Wars much as the Persian poet had been a
contemporary of Tamburlaine and his campaigns. In the private sphere,
Goethe had a new late passion, and his humorous yet tender play with motifs
and names from a distant culture was apt for what could never be more than
a poetic courtship – Marianne Willemer was married, Goethe was a friend of
the family. Remarkably, it appears Marianne wrote a handful of poems in
reply to his which were fine enough to be included in the *Divan* and to keep
the secret of their authorship till long after Goethe's death.

Hatem   1815   (p. 35)

This is consciously a poem addressed by an old grey-haired lover to a young
beloved, and it confronts that insuperable difference ruefully but playfully.
(These adverbs can be reversed.) He laments that he has nothing to offer in
return for her beauty, made graphically real in the locks of hair that hold him
captive close to her face; but then he realises there is one thing that age has
left undiminished, which is his strength of feeling. He presses this point in
the time-honoured imagery of fire, first with a grand hyperbole – his heart is
an Etna whose raging heat belies the mountain's cold grey exterior, and may
even break out alarmingly ('rast...dir hervor' virtually brings the lava to her
feet!) – and then with an outright comic exaggeration, perhaps inspired by
the wine he has been drinking: the consuming flames of passion may literally
achieve just that, through the spontaneous combustion of the lover. The poem

has moved from a moment of intimate physical closeness, through elaborate word-games, back to the woman it started from. Her brief matter-of-fact words have the cool neutrality of a 'belle dame sans merci'. Imagined as they are by the poet-lover, they are a final touch of rueful self-mockery.

stanza 1: 'Schlangen' may seem a disturbing image (memories of the Medusa's snake-locks). Or has it been transformed into an image of attraction?

stanza 3: Why does 'Hatem' fail to rhyme with 'Morgenröte'?

Suleika 1815   **(p. 36)**

Attributed to Marianne. Separation is a fundamental motif, and motive, of love poetry. It naturally generates wistful images of connection. Distant lovers agree to look up at the moon and think of one another at the same time every night (cf. *Dem aufgehenden Vollmonde*, p. 47); similarly, they think of the winds blowing between them as a kind of communication. In another of Marianne's poems, *Was bedeutet die Bewegung?*, Suleika's heart is soothed when she feels the East wind is bringing her Hatem's greetings and kisses. Now she envies the West wind which can go back to him, carrying the message of what she is suffering in his absence. The motif of the rain that the West wind typically carries (ll. 1 and 7f) mingles with the motif of tears, human emotion becomes part of nature – 'Blumen, Augen, Wald und Hügel' – as in *Maifest* and *Fetter grüne du Laub*. Suffering is balanced by hope (st. 3) and she changes her mind about what word to send (st. 4). Instead of making much of her troubles, a more modest ('bescheiden'), yet a fundamental message: to be near him again will make her feel not just love but life itself more intensely.

line 10: für Leid = vor Leid

line 17: some editions have the comma after 'aber'. Goethe was reworking a draft that read 'Sag ihm nur, doch sag's bescheiden'.

Einlaß 1820   **(p. 36)**

This playful dialogue, from the enlarged (1827) *Divan*, serves serious ends. It allows the poet a wrily triumphant look at his past, its hard knocks and achievements, it becomes the record of a life, a philosophy of life. But the charm is in the play. The houri on duty at the gates of paradise (a sexier version of St Peter) thinks this non-Moslem is a dubious candidate for admittance by normal Islamic standards. Has he a good fighting record, with wounds to prove it? Is he 'really related' to 'our' Moslems (ll. 5f)? He airily waves away her doubts, and links autobiography with a typically Enlightenment humanism (l. 15) in an answer that overarches religious difference: the simple fact of being a 'Mensch', and the common need to struggle which that entails, make all human beings related. (Rychner, p. 557, documents the idea of 'life as struggle' from biblical, Greek and Latin sources.) His own struggles have left him with wounds from love and war; but still nothing ever undid his faith in the world or stopped him singing its praises. With no false modesty he claims to have collaborated with the outstanding people and made a name with the tenderest hearts of his day: it is no nonentity she will be letting in. He presumes on her favourable decision, and in the last lines is already pressing, with a delightfully discreet but suggestive image, for the pleasures Islam promises the faithful.

Urworte. Orphisch   1817   (p. 38)

Goethe had been following a scholars' controversy over myth, in particular over the theory that there had been an original Asian or Egyptian religion of which ancient Greek mythology was allegedly already a late version. As a devotee still of classical Greece, Goethe was reluctant to see its clear images and concepts dissolved in murky mysticism and speculation (letter of 1 October 1817 to Creuzer).

   Urworte. Orphisch sets out to give a wholly unmystical account of the forces determining human life. 'Orphisch' alludes to the archetypal poet-figure Orpheus, who, though Greek, was himself the centre of a quasi-mystical cult. So Goethe may have meant the word as more of an irony than an acknowledgement. The other element in the title certainly stresses his independence of the Orphic tradition. Where the alleged Orphic writings were referred to as 'sacred words' ('ιεροι λογοι'), the term 'Urworte' makes no sacral claims: it simply means 'original' or 'fundamental words'. These may generate maxims for living, but are in no narrow sense religious. One of Goethe's impulses as a scientist had been to discover fundamental phenomena, an 'Urpflanze', an 'Urtier' – an 'Urphänomen' in whatever field – which shaped the individual species through metamorphosis. In the same spirit, he now surveys the equally fundamental influences that shape the individual life. (That the poem was first published, in 1820, in his journal *Zur Morphologie*, confirms the connection with his scientific thinking.) The concepts are however not original to Goethe. They are found in Greek and apparently also in ancient Egyptian thought. In 1789 Goethe's friend Knebel had written a poem about the first four of them (reprinted Eibl 2, 1093). It would not be worth comparing this modest piece with Goethe's, except that it brings out the effect of his added fifth force. Knebel's poem, ending with 'necessity' ('die Not'), has a necessarily downbeat ending: though fate may give with one hand, it takes away with the other. Indeed, a logical conclusion to the sequence of fundamental forces, as Kommerell points out (p. 201), might well be 'death'. Goethe, as in so many other contexts, ends upbeat, on hope. Perhaps he has in mind the myth of Pandora's box according to which, despite all the evils that had been released into the world, humanity was still left with hope.

(Pandora will recur in the *Trilogie der Leidenschaft*. See *Elegie* ll. 135f, p. 45.)

Describing the field of forces that affects all human beings equally is bound to involve general statement. Yet the language of Goethe's poem is paradoxically not abstract. It is worth checking through and classifying its vocabulary. For a start, there are none of the abstractions commonly found in philosophical parlance – no nouns in '-heit', '-keit', '-nis', only one in '-ung', and that one not abstruse but almost concrete in meaning: 'Bedingung'. Instead, simple words and familiar images embody the interplay of the grand forces and make them graspable: 'Tag', 'Welt', 'Zeit', 'Macht', 'Form', 'Grenze', 'Mauer', 'Tand', 'Lampe', 'Flamme', 'Wohl', 'Weh', 'Wille', 'Herz', 'Stirn', 'Brust', etc. We see the forces in action through a succession of verbs, which are the most dynamic part of speech; while such abstract nouns as do occur are themselves mostly nominalised forms of some part of a verb: 'ein Wandelndes' (st. 2), 'vom Fliehen' (st. 3), 'dem harten Muß' (st. 4). Everything suggests movement and metamorphosis. Finally, to bring all this home to us, the poem sets a very personal scene in sts. 1 and 2 by addressing a 'du' (the reader or/and the reflecting poet himself – the usual ambiguity); and he maintains that feeling in sts. 4 and 5 by moving on to the solidarity of 'wir' and 'uns', which is more a development from 'du' than an inconsistency.

Yet along with that sense of the movement and fluidity of life's processes, Goethe's *ottava rima* stanza has a monumental mass that adds a note of authority. And though there are transitions between the stanzas, most strikingly 'Die bleibt nicht aus' at l. 19, each one is a complete and separate account of one force, with the final couplet rounding off the argument: all there was to say about that force has been said. Stanza by stanza, the individual life moves organically on to the next internal or external challenge.

For this, as for a number of poems he thought difficult for readers, Goethe provided his own stanza-by-stanza commentary. It is reprinted in full in HA 1, 403ff and in Staiger 2, 487ff.

Heading: 'Dämon'. Not demonic possession, but the distinctive inner nature of the individual, character as fate. 'Der alte Adam' is one of Goethe's paraphrases in his commentary.

lines 1f: 'verliehen', supply 'hat'. The opening of Goethe's autobiography, *Dichtung und Wahrheit*, makes much of the planetary positions at the time of his own birth.

line 6: 'Sibyllen und Propheten'. The sooth-sayers respectively of Classical Antiquity and the Judaic world. They were juxtaposed in Raphael's paintings in the Sistine Chapel in Rome, which Goethe saw and admired in 1786. In the first printing, this line read: 'Das ändern nicht Sibyllen, nicht Propheten'.

line 7: Instead of 'Macht', that first printing read 'Kraft'.

line 13: 'hin- und widerfällig'. 'Hinfällig' here not in its usual sense of 'feeble', 'not valid', but used inventively to mean 'falling out our way', i.e., favourably. The whole phrase thus means 'sometimes things go your way, sometimes not'.

line 14: 'Tand...durch getandelt'. Inventive again, this time making up a verb from the noun that is its object (i.e., a cognate verb, as in 'to live one's life'). Roughly, 'the worthless stuff of social life is given the routine treatment'.

line 17: 'Die...Er'. Respectively 'Flamme', and 'Eros' – love personified as a god.

line 18: 'aus alter Öde'. Eros, mythically, arose out of primordial Chaos.

line 20: 'den Frühlingstag'. Allegorical for the whole time of youth.

line 23f: 'im Allgemeinen...dem Einen'. Suggests sexual roving as against fidelity in love. Goethe's commentary extends it to the family as the basis of ordered society.

line 32: 'nur enger dran'. Typical of the colloquial note that is never far away in Goethe, this time helping to authenticate general wisdom with the ring of individual experience. In a letter of 16 July 1818 to Boisserée, he says that his poem 'die abgestorbenen Redensarten aus eigener Erfahrungs-Lebendigkeit wieder anfrischt'.

line 33: 'ehrnen Mauer'. 'Ehern' as usual in the sense of hard realities, and as usual with the idea they can be overcome. Cf. note on p. 80 to *Das Göttliche*, l. 32.

line 35: 'sie stehe nur' = 'even if it stands'.

line 40: 'ein Flügelschlag'. Hope, such is its power, seems not even to need a verb to help us cast off the burden of the ages.

St Nepomuks Vorabend   1820 (p. 39)

St Nepomuk was the confessor of a fourteenth-century Bohemian queen. He refused to break the seal of confession as demanded by her husband the king, who had him drowned in the Moldau. According to the legend, his body floated downstream miraculously accompanied by lights. Goethe was present in 1820 at the yearly memorial ceremony, when lighted candles are launched on to the river. The poem is as much evocation as description, achieved through the simple language and unforced compression that are typical of Goethe's late lyric. Typical too is the casual reshaping of words and syntax, for example the deviant form 'Brücken' in l. 2 and 'Fehle' in l. 8, presumably the never-used plural of the archaic 'Fehl'; and in l. 3 the pairing of 'Glocke, Glöckchen' without any 'und', the noun modulating into its diminutive, and the two then taking a singular verb. That makes them at once a single object, an incantation, and an echo of bells: not a display of violence done to language, as in the young poet's dramatic monologues, but an ingenuity that unobtrusively creates atmosphere and mood. The poet is plainly touched by goodness, death and commemoration, even if he does not share the religious faith in which the legend is rooted. This is just about the extent of Goethe's rapprochement with Romantic medievalism into which his friendship with the Boisserée brothers had drawn him.

The imperatives in the final stanza, like those of *Im Herbst 1775* (see p. 19), simultaneously evoke and assent to what they record, here the sights and sounds of the ceremony. The last line, perhaps starting from the lights and their reflection in the water, suggests not so much Catholic canonisation as the pagan notion that a chosen being is placed as a new star among the constellations.

Parabase 1820 (p. 39)

First published untitled, then with this title in the 'Gott und Welt' section of the poems in the 1827 'Ausgabe letzter Hand', in between longer scientific poems. Hence the title, which is a term from Greek comedy meaning 'comments addressed to the audience, interrupting the action'.

What starts as an informal, almost chatty recollection of Goethe's long experience as a scientist quickly turns into a dense yet lucid evocation of nature's workings. Aptly and crucially, the poem opens with simple verbs. A prose retrospect might have fallen into a noun phrase like 'langjährige naturwissenschaftliche Bemühungen' – formal and fixed; but the phrase 'zu erforschen, zu erfahren' is fluid, two verbs of action introducing an indirect question – 'wie' – that in turn leads on to the dynamic process Goethe has always intuitively grasped: that nature is continually creating new forms out of the same basic materials. 'Im Schaffen lebt' is already far from a normal prose formulation; it prepares the sharp rise in poetic temperature of the lines that follow. The present tense ('lebt') suggests that Goethe's conception is still going strong.

The simple opening 'Und' in l. 5 conveys an expectation duly fulfilled and insights unveiled as we move into the detail of how nature operates. Yet the world's workings can hardly be fitted into the remaining eight lines. On the other hand, eight lines are far more than is needed for the abstract statement that 'nature endlessly recycles forms and materials'. What the poem offers, between the two extremes of unmanageable detail and bald reduction, is an incantatory play with opposed terms each of which embodies one aspect, either material or formal, of nature's processes: the eternal as against its temporal shapes; unity against multiplicity; large and small; change and permanence; near and far. These terms are themselves abstract and general, yet they are made to seem concrete and almost visible as participants in a

dance of forces that brings about nature's transformations. Even l. 10, where
the reversal of 'Nah und fern' into 'fern und nah' adds no new meaning, is
itself an instance of transformation. The whole culminates and is summed up
in the formula 'so gestaltend, umgestaltend'.

Who or what exactly is the agent of all these processes? 'Das ewig Eine'
– nature, or God – has already been invoked. All the phrases from l. 9
onwards, suggestive though they are of an aesthetic and near-mystical delight
that goes beyond rational statement, are waiting for a grammatical subject to
pick up that idea and answer the ultimate question. The adjectives and, espe-
cially, the four active participles build up expectancy – but then the sentence
breaks off with a dash, no grammatical subject, and no answer; and the poem
ends instead with a simple statement of wonder. This is not so much because
language cannot stretch any further, but because thinking once more about
nature's processes has renewed the feeling of wonder yet again. It is the
impulse from which all Goethe's scientific work started, and it is more im-
portant than that work and the insights it achieved. To wonder at nature rather
than to investigate it is the purpose of his existence – l. 12 states Goethe's
priorities very clearly. By breaking off where it does, the poem acts on them.

Trilogie der Leidenschaft   1823/24   (p. 40)

Goethe gave the three poems about his last love this title, and put them in this
order, for the 'Ausgabe letzter Hand' in 1827. He wrote them in the reverse
order: *Aussöhnung* was the response to a crisis that had not yet fully unfolded;
Elegie then treated it exhaustively; and *An Werther*, written last, became its
prelude after the event.

Aussöhnung, a celebration of the soothing power of music, was inspired
by the playing of the Polish pianist Marie Szymanowska and written while
Goethe was still at the Bohemian spa-town of Marienbad, where it all
happened. The trilogy's centrepiece, *Elegie*, sometimes known as the
'Marienbad Elegy', is his one truly unhappy love-poem. 'Unhappy' is indeed
an understatement. The frustration of a late passion – at seventy-four he
seriously wanted to marry the eighteen-year-old Ulrike von Levetzow –
reduced more than just his emotional life to ruins. It destabilised his whole
sense of himself and his place in the world; his activities lost their point; his
positive vision of life was reversed.

Elegie looks back over the affair from its end-point, a moment of hope
(sts. 1-3) quickly extinguished (sts. 4, 5). It tries to escape from memories
into the wider world (st. 6), but even there cannot get away from her image
(st. 7). So instead it seeks to remember her even more, and more exactly,
evoking the happy times and the rejuvenating effect of love in an extended
flashback that is the core of the poem (sts. 8-18). Eventually it returns to the

unhappy present moment (sts. 19-21) with the poet returning to Weimar. (Typically of Goethe's creative processes, the first drafts were scribbled in an old diary, often in near-final formulation, as the coach carried him home.) At the end he says farewell to his old companions, his old scientific attachment to the world, and his old belief that he was a favoured being (sts. 22, 23). The very last line is abrupt and unmitigatedly bleak.

The only mitigation lies in the poem's motto, words perhaps called to mind by the phrasing of l. 104. It is a quotation from an earlier work of Goethe's, the drama *Torquato Tasso* of 1790, at the near-tragic end of which the Italian poet takes comfort from his ability to express what he suffers. In setting Tasso's climactic statement before the *Elegie* in the fair copy he made immediately he got back to Weimar in September 1823, Goethe was giving his tragic poem a rescuing function that had been nowhere explicit within the text itself. Read in this light, the *Elegie* may begin to seem less bleak. The mere fact of writing means that passion is no longer passive, and the finished poem has at least taken the measure of misery. Raw misery is now recorded misery; the sufferer can hold it at arm's length for inspection, or alternatively he can press it to him and renew the pain, in the hope that this may cure it. Goethe did actually have the poem read and re-read to him by his friend Zelter like some personal liturgy.

Some months later Goethe was about to republish the tragic novel of his youth, *Die Leiden des jungen Werthers*, fifty years after its first appearance. It was an unjubilant jubilee: the classic of despairing love was too close to the quick of his recent unhappiness. Instead of the new introduction his publisher had requested, Goethe wrote *An Werther*. Its message is summed up in the terrible words that condone the hero's suicide, the more bitter for their colloquial phrasing: 'Gingst du voran – und hast nicht viel verloren'. Having looked with a cold eye on departure and separation, death, and the illusory value of life, the poem ends with only the slightest upturn, the notion that torment may find a crumb of comfort in utterance; but even this, with the hollow echo of the internal rhyme 'meiden/Scheiden' (l. 48), sounds more sceptical, even sarcastic, than convinced.

Yet the wording plainly foreshadows the motto of the *Elegie* which, in the trilogy layout, is what we read next. There is thus a conflict between that deliberate arrangement and the actual sequence of emotions and responses in the poet's experience. In the arrangement, negativity is overcome; in life, it was the final stage. Thus even when the individual poems were finished, they were still raw material for the poetic structure. The choice was between tragic fact and non-tragic art, between letting the final dark mood prevail – *An Werther* is even darker than *Elegie*, because it is not a cry of immediate anguish but a considered nihilistic statement – and somehow putting it in a perspective that could be lived with.

Once Goethe had opted for the non-tragic emphasis, it was paradoxically strengthened by *An Werther*. Placed in first position, the harsh utterance became itself another crisis overcome – by the other two poems. Moreover, the double retrospect, on a novel and a drama that had clear affinities with each other (Goethe later approved a French critic's *aperçu* that Tasso was an intensified Werther – in conversation with his amanuensis Eckermann, 3 May 1827) and with the new crisis, put the Elegy in perspective. It created a context of general principle (this is what poetry can do) and of personal history (this is what it *has* done in two past crises). The two earlier works become a home-made mythology Goethe can draw on for support. The final ordering of the poems in the trilogy declares he has successfully done that.

Aussöhnung was meant to put the finishing touch. In any other context it would not seem a slight poem. It risks seeming so only in the company of *An Werther* and *Elegie*, whether we read them as coming before it in the printed sequence and setting an unreachable standard, or as coming after it in the sequence of events and responses and outdoing this first, altogether gentler poem. The fact that Madame Szymanowska again played the piano for Goethe in Weimar in the November of 1823 is not enough (*pace* Eibl 2, 1057) to bring the chronology into line with the printed trilogy – *An Werther*, after all, had yet to be written. Much less can it undo the force of textual comparison. The language of the other two poems has plumbed (or, viewed genetically, had yet to plumb) greater depths. A good starting-point for comparing poetic effect is where Goethe has used the same rhymes: 'erkoren/verloren' in *An Werther*, ll. 9f and *Aussöhnung*, ll. 2 and 4; 'Sehnen/Tränen' in *Elegie*, ll. 113f and *Aussöhnung*, 11f.

But *Aussöhnung* did crucially prepare the six-line stanza form and rhyme-scheme that Goethe was to use in *Elegie* (though it appears he started on a different tack: of what is now st. 1, he at first wrote only ll. 1, 3, 5 and 6, making two couplets, which did not even necessarily point to any kind of stanza at all). The rhyme-scheme is a main source of the trilogy's power, building up emotional suspense through lines rhymed *abab* ('Kreuzreim'), then releasing it in a concluding couplet (*cc*). The same pattern holds for *An Werther*, though here the stanzas vary in length (10, 10, 6, 6, 6 and 12 lines) and hence in the number of 'Kreuzreime' preparing each conclusion. Goethe had already used this form – eight-line ottava rima or its six-line variant – in philosophical poems, for example in the never completed humanist allegory *Die Geheimnisse*, in its dedicatory poem *Zueignung* which he later placed as the preface to all his collections of lyric (neither of these poems is included in the present volume), and in *Urworte. Orphisch*. It is clear that this stanza is well suited to laying out arguments and offering a resolution. The impression of conclusiveness, even inexorability, might seem at first sight unsuited to a love theme. Yet arguably that impression does fit the bitter lament for a lost and last love, and for the seeming end to all life's savour.

An Werther (p. 40)

line 1: 'vielbeweinter Schatten'. Goethe's novel was a sensation, and Werther became a much-mourned cult figure.

line 13: 'Paradieses Wonne'. The initial brief happy state. The unfolding pattern of human life that Goethe evokes in these stanzas is similar, though darker in tone, to the one he presents in *Urworte. Orphisch*. The return to paradise through love, and the exclusion from paradise through its loss, are motifs in *Elegie* (ll. 3, 5, 7; and 21-24).

line 40: 'gräßlich Scheiden'. Werther's bungled suicide; he shoots himself, but dies a long drawn out death.

lines 45f: The sentence tails away, unfinished and brooding. Supply some such word as 'bestimmt' ('destined to...').

Elegie (p. 41)

Motto: 'was ich leide'. The wording in the play *Torquato Tasso* is '*wie* ich leide'. The change may have been inadvertent, and may not be significant. Only a fine line separates the substance and the manner of suffering.

line 5: If the house where she receives him is to be called 'Paradies' (l. 7), then 'Himmelstor' is simply a metaphorical description of its entrance. It in no way suggests (*pace* Witte, **GHb**, p. 484) that she is thought of as dead.

lines 5f: 'Tor...empor'. The only closing couplet with masculine rhymes in the whole trilogy is also the highpoint of envisioned happiness.

line 11: 'dieses...Schönen', neuter not feminine. For all the sexual interest, her beauty means far more than sexual attraction, as the rest of the poem will show.

line 20: 'Minne' is a medieval word for courtly love, in which the woman was idealised and worshipped from afar.

lines 21ff: The cherub with the flaming sword and the expulsion from Paradise echo the Bible story of the Fall (Genesis 3: 24). Adam, of course, was not driven out alone; Eve went with him.

line 24f: 'verschlossen./Und nun verschlossen...' Picking up the thread by using the same word with a different sense links the stanzas and turns the narrative in a new direction. This is typical of the poem's tautness and coherence. Cf. the transition at ll. 66f, 'Und zwar durch sie!'

lines 31ff: Turning his mind to the outside world is foiled when cloud-shapes recall her graceful figure. The attempt to escape his obsession is seemingly forgotten, and replaced by an active pursuit of remembrance (ll. 45ff).

line 57: 'seiner eignen Dauer'. Cf. p. 35 'Locken, haltet mich', l. 5.

line 65: 'begeistet'. Not 'begeistert', enthused, but an invention of Goethe's meaning 'turned into spirit', something like a sublimation process, since it dissolved even the need for an answering love (ll. 61f).

line 74: 'wir lesen's'. Philippians 4: 7 (quoted above, p. 70). The phrase is casual, almost dismissive, a matter of taking cognisance, not of believing. What Goethe develops out of the Pauline conception, by equating the 'peace that passeth all understanding' with the happiness of earthly love, is correspondingly far from orthodox.

lines 79ff: '...fromm sein'. Goethe's idea of piety is just as unorthodox. It is a late form of Enlightenment deism, a reverence for the world that avoids the opposed extremes of scientific materialism and religious dogmatism: the piety of a poet and a visionary scientist.

lines 91ff: 'als wenn sie sagte'. Even allowing for the hypothetical 'als wenn', this transferring of the poet's own philosophy of life to his eighteen-year-old beloved, as a way of saying that love confirmed him in it, is arguably the poem's weakest point.

line 112: 'mich ihm entschlagen': 'relinquish', 'get rid of it'. Normally with the genitive (see Note to *Sag, was könnt' uns Mandarinen* p. 103).

lines 129-132: 'Nur immer zu...' These lines manage to convey the range of knowledge and depth of pleasure that science had given Goethe, while making clear only by the twist in the very last word, the bitter invention 'nachgestammelt', that this happiness too has lost its meaning.

line 133: 'Mir ist...verloren': cf. Tasso's penultimate speech in the last scene of *Torquato Tasso* after he has alienated the Princess: 'Ist alles denn verloren? [...] Nein, es ist alles da und ich bin nichts;/ Ich bin mir selbst entwandt, sie ist es mir'.

lines 135f: 'Pandoren...Gefahr'. This alters the myth, according to which Pandora's box contained not good things but evils, and when her husband Epimetheus (Prometheus' brother) unwisely opened it, they were all let out. Even more significantly, there is no mention of hope being left as mankind's sole consolation. (Cf. Note to *Urworte. Orphisch* p. 91f.)

line 137: 'drängten... gabeseligen Munde'. This powerful metaphor for a life of happiness and privilege also picks up the leitmotif of her embrace and kisses (ll. 6, 19, 51f).

Aussöhnung (p. 45)

line 1: 'Leidenschaft...Leiden'. Not quite an aphorism, and a touch obvious and lightweight after the shattering close of *Elegie*; but it links the trilogy's title with that of the novel, *Die Leiden des jungen Werthers*.

Im ernsten Beinhaus war's 1827 (p. 46)

The skull this poem contemplates is Schiller's. The great dramatist, poet, historian, aesthetic philosopher and literary critic had been Goethe's friend and collaborator during the intensively productive decade known as Weimar Classicism (1794-1805). For Goethe, Schiller's early death at forty-six was a heavy blow. In 1827 the vault where he had been buried was cleared out, and while the remains waited to be reinterred, Goethe for a time kept Schiller's skull at home. The poem's situation is thus close to life, though it is not known that Goethe ever actually stood in the charnel-house surveying the bones of Schiller's neighbours in death.

A skull is the classic reminder of mortality, an object of sobering meditation found in both ancient and Christian poetry and art. Its owner is not usually identified, it is a general emblem of a universal fate. Where the identity is known, the horror can be all the greater. In the famous scene where Hamlet contemplates Yorick's skull (Goethe must have had it at the back of his mind when writing his poem) every observed detail recalls yet also devalues the vanished life. Hamlet remembers the jester's jollity, but his 'gorge rises at it' – at the memories of life, be it noted, not just at the skull itself (Act V, sc. 1, circa l. 180). Yorick might as well not have been.

Goethe resists any such second annihilation of Schiller. He celebrates individuality in more than memory, asserting against the common fate the distinctive trace that persists in the very bone. Not however before he has faced death in all the grim impersonality of the crowded charnel-house. That is surely why he sets the scene there and not in the seeming safety of a human dwelling, where he would have been alone with his friend's skull. He also imagines with total unsentimentality how in life the owners of these bones hated and killed one another (ll. 4f), and he does no more than hint at vanished grace (l. 8) and noble capacities (l. 12). There is little reason so far for not sharing Hamlet's revulsion: nobody can love 'die dürre Schale' that remains (l. 13).

But the poet turns out to be this Nobody. His argument pivots on the 'Doch' of l. 15 and on his claim to be an initiate ('mir Adepten') who can 'read' the skull. Love, implicitly, *is* possible to the eye of knowledge: to the osteologist, the observer sensitised to the diversity of human forms, the scientist who can place human variety in its turn within the natural continuum; and to the poet and friend who knew and recognises Schiller. Unlike the Yorick scene, there is a sense that the spirit and its housing are connected by more than the contingent fact of being alive, and that the housing need not be an object of abhorrence. It is the ultimate test of Goethe's 'loving realism' (cf. Introduction, p. xvf).

Schiller's mortal remnant is not the only beneficiary, passively waiting to be rehabilitated by the poet. It offers him a powerful inspiration in return. This comes first from the thought of Schiller's creativity. The mode is not lament ('Alas! poor Schiller, I knew him') but paean: 'What incalculable splendour (l. 18), what a source of life (l. 21) was and is in Schiller! Am I fit to hold so great a treasure as the bone that contained his spirit?'(l. 27f). A yet larger inspiration then transports him in imagination to an ocean-flood of forces that is constantly generating new forms – a dynamic counter-image to the inert mass of bones with which the poem began. Inspiration becomes vision, vision becomes a quasi-religious revelation, already hinted at in l. 16 ('heil'gen Sinn... offenbarte') and culminating in l. 32 where 'Gott-Natur' reveals itself. The poem is more than just a rejection of death's dominion; it becomes the liturgy of a personal faith – humanist, deist or pantheist – for which Schiller's skull is a sacred relic. 'Schillers Reliquien' is indeed what Goethe privately called the poem (letter of 24 October 1827 to Zelter). Its message, close to that of *Dauer im Wechsel*, is that 'Gott-Natur' transmutes human substance into spirit, but also preserves spirit as a new substance. One further religious association is the *terza rima* form, rare in German and only ever used once elsewhere by Goethe (the opening scene of *Faust II* (ll. 4679-4727). It is the form of the great Catholic poem of heaven and hell, Dante's *Divine Comedy*, which in 1827 had recently been translated into German by Karl Streckfuss.

In sum, Goethe has taken on the materials and literary tradition of musings on death and contrived a poem that celebrates life, 'als ob' (in the poem's own words) 'ein Lebensquell dem Tod entspränge'.

line 1: 'Im...war's'. Already a strong emphasis (cf. a neutral formulation, e.g. 'Ich stand im ernsten Beinhaus, und da sah ich'): the revelation happened in this of all places where you would expect to have only gloomy experiences, giving rise to the intimations of mortality normal in devotional poetry and Christian homily.

line 2: 'Schädel Schädeln'. The second word is in the dative, going with 'angeordnet'. Pushing the two 'skulls' against each other with no other word between (contrast, as might be, 'Wie Schädel eng bei andern Schädeln lagen') makes the words visibly and aurally enact the dense crush they describe.

line 4: 'stehn in Reih'. Packing words in so there is not enough room for their full form ('stehen in Reihe[n]') gets much the same effect as l. 2.

lines 7, 9: 'die Hand, der Fuß'. Cf. the detached contemplation of parts of the body in sts. 3 and 4 of *Dauer im Wechsel*; there they were constantly changing, here they are fixed in their last form.

line 9: 'aus Lebensfugen'. Conceivably an echo of another much-quoted line from *Hamlet*, 'The time is out of joint; O cursèd spite/ That ever I was born to set it right' (Act I, sc. v, 189f); in German 'Die Zeit ist aus den Fugen'.

lines 11f: 'Nicht Ruh im Grabe'. An ironic echo of the conventional prayer 'Rest in peace', since these bones have not been allowed to.

line 15: 'Adepten'. Originally one initiated into the secrets of alchemy, an interest of Goethe's youth. Behind it, more specifically, lies Goethe's interest and participation in the 'physiognomic' studies of his friend Johann Caspar Lavater in the 1770s. Since then scientific attention had shifted from facial types to skull types, through the work of a later acquaintance, Franz Josef Gall. (As early as 1804, a follower of Gall's wrote a study of the relation of Kant's skull to his brain.)

line 23: 'gottgedachte Spur'. A God with consciousness – i.e., not just the forces of Nature personified – is invoked at least for poetic purposes. Cf. the poem 'Es ist gut' in the *West-östlicher Divan*, where the beloved is addressed as 'Liebster von allen Gottes-Gedanken'.

line 25: 'gesteigerte Gestalten'. Possibly Schiller's dramatic characters, but more probably the manifold forms nature generates.

line 26: 'Orakelsprüche'. Again, possibly Schiller's own utterances, but more probably the ideas about 'Gott-Natur' that this meditation on his skull gives rise to.

lines 28ff: 'Schatz...fromm entwendend'. 'Stealing' a 'highest treasure' is paradoxically a pious action ('fromm'), and taking it out into the free air and light a reverent act or act of worship ('andächtig').

line 33: 'das Feste...zu Geist verrinnen'. The words have very specific reference to Schiller, who ruined his physical health by overwork.

On its first appearance, placed at the end of Goethe's novel *Wilhelm Meisters Wanderjahre* in 1829 (the poetry volumes of the 'Ausgabe letzter Hand' having already been published) the poem was followed by the words 'Ist fortzusetzen'. A manuscript does indeed exist with some inchoate lines of *terza rima* (printed by Eibl 2, 1201) which could be a sketch for such a continuation, especially as the lines refer to 'der Freund'. Perhaps, as Eibl conjectures, Goethe thought of writing a cycle of poems celebrating Schiller.

Chinesisch-deutsche Jahres- und Tageszeiten 1827

Goethe explored Chinese poetry and culture as he earlier had Persian, though not at such length or to such depth, and produced a cycle of fourteen short poems.

I Sag, was könnt' uns Mandarinen (p. 47)

It was not hard for Goethe to slip into the imagined situation of an old mandarin, a member of the cultivated class that governed ancient China, who is tired of administration and can now relax with the remaining pleasures of the flesh and the spirit. That virtually *was* Goethe's situation. Add to which the domestic fact that he was spending much time in his 'Gartenhaus', the tiny dwelling by the River Ilm where he had lived when he first came to Weimar. Old age necessarily brought with it the question 'what is left?' As with other life-questions that commonly imply gloomy answers, Goethe's response is positive without being glibly optimistic.

line 5: 'Uns des Nordens zu entschlagen'. Literally: 'to get rid of the north', that is, to care no more about the responsibilities of administration (Peking means 'northern capital').

VIII Dämmrung senkte sich von oben   (p. 47)

An evocation of the play of darkness and light on water as night falls and the stars and moon appear. Perhaps, behind that, a hint of the greater darkness that threatens old age, offset by the comfort of moonlight – but this is at most suggested, not asserted, as in the delicate symbolism of oriental lyric.

line 4: 'holden Lichts' = 'with its lovely light'. Such genitive adjectival or adverbial phrases are a stylistic thumb-print of the older Goethe, an unobtrusive means to achieve compression. It does so by a measurable margin, as against the formulation 'mit seinem holden Licht'. But the device feels entirely idiomatic, being structurally identical with standard phrases like 'schweren Herzens' or 'guten Willens'. For other examples see below, the two Dornburg poems (p. 104).

line 7: 'schwarzvertiefte...'. An equally typical invention.

line 12: 'nächsten Flut'. 'Nächst' cannot here be temporal, so this would mean 'the part of the water's surface nearest the speaker'. There is something to be said for the suggested emendation 'nächt'gen Flut'.

IX Nun weiß man erst was Rosenknospe sei   (p. 48)

Almost too simple to need, or allow, comment. Which is not to say that the emotion it describes is simple, as becomes clear when you try to paraphrase it.

For example, in l. 4: 'ergänzt' literally means 'completes'. The sense here has been much discussed (cf. Eibl 2, 1217). Like the bud itself, the word contains a lot in a little. A single and last rose-bud makes good the absence of all other flowers, suggests them, conjures them up for our imagination, makes us appreciate what we no longer have, and more besides. It is a physical symbol for the garden visitor, a verbal symbol for the reader – a poetic 'Urpflanze'.

Wenn im Unendlichen dasselbe 1827   (p. 48)

A number of late poems, mostly grouped in the 'Gott und Welt' section of the 'Ausgabe letzter hand', sum up the vision of the world Goethe had achieved over a long lifetime by the exercise of a scientific mind and a poetic sensibility that were not kept separate. It is a vision of continual movement and change which, however far science has progressed since Goethe's day, is essentially in tune with modern thinking in the life- and earth-sciences, from plant genetics to plate tectonics to chaos theory.

The longer poems of that group – *Eins und Alles, Vermächtnis* – are powerful and exhaustive statements, their phrasing often memorable in the way maxims are memorable. They do indeed turn Goethe's perception of dynamic reality into a set of maxims to live by: willing integration of the individual in the totality of nature; constant self-adaptation to guard against inertia and inflexibility; trust in a constantly moving yet ordered universe, trust in human conscience, trust in the evidence of our senses; enjoyment of a present that can symbolically contain both past and future; and robust independence of mind to avoid conformism.

If these longer poems are didactic in manner, Goethe's imagination – true to the principles just sketched – remains generally mobile and flexible. He can still catch wisdom on the wing in moments of live insight and create an image whose coherence is poetic rather than discursive. The brief poem *Wenn im Unendlichen* contains the essence of his vision. It captures in similar brief compass to *Parabase* the movement, strength, delight, and ultimate stability of the universe. It also in a remarkable way parallels his earliest poetic perceptions as captured in *Maifest*. In both there is a pulsating activity, a 'Dringen' or 'Drängen', which is driven by a similar force of delight, 'Liebe' or 'Lebenslust', within a similar overarching system, 'die herrlich leuchte[nde] Natur' or 'das tausendfältige Gewölbe'. Not surprisingly, the passage of sixty years has shifted the emphasis from the sheer exuberance of life's forces to the patterns of recurrence they flow in (l. 2) and the ultimate calm (l. 8) that their intense activity composes. But it is recognisably the same world, and the poetic response to it is as consistent as it is fresh. (Cf. Introduction, p. viiif.)

The Dornburg poems

In summer and autumn 1828, after the death of Carl August in June, Goethe spent two months at the idyllic castle of Dornburg near Weimar. He was mainly occupied studying plants and making meteorological observations, his mood overshadowed by the loss of his employer and friend of over fifty years.

Dem aufgehenden Vollmonde   1828   (p. 48)

Goethe sent this poem to Marianne Willemer in October 1828. It renews the lovers' custom from *Divan* days by which they would each look at the moon at a given time in the knowledge that the other would be doing the same. Here the moon is at first only an intermittent helper, perhaps in line with its proverbial inconstancy. But the frustration of st. 1 is eased in st. 2 where a fragment of the moon's rim is visible above the cloud, like a star – the constancy of stars as a guide is equally proverbial. In the third stanza, the moon emerges from cloud completely, and the sky is like a clean-swept road ('Bahn'): a visual and an emotional highpoint. As in *Dämmrung senkte sich von oben*, light overcomes darkness. Despite the speaker's pain, the mood is almost triumphal.

stanza 1: three lines of literally childlike simplicity, with one (l. 3) of the old Goethe's casually inventive compressions ('umfinstern') thrown in.

line 9: the now familiar imperative of delighted assent, this time with the actual verb only implied by the directional prefix ('hinan').

line 10: 'Reiner Bahn'. Again the genitive adverbial phrase serves compression.

line 11: 'schlägt mein Herz auch' = 'wenn auch mein Herz...' ('even if...'). In the version sent to Marianne, this line read 'schneller, schneller'.

line 12: 'überselig'. The meaning is surely not an excess but, unusually, an extreme – 'supremely blissful'.

Dornburg, September 1828 (p. 49)

A day-poem exactly balancing – in form too – the night-poem, with a stanza for each of three times of day. Reading the evocation of early morning in st. 1 is like seeing a black-and-white image turn coloured before our eyes. Then, as in the night-poem, a brief struggle with cloud leaves a clear sky: 'Bahn' again suggesting spaciousness and release. But the third stanza evokes a future, not an actual sunset. The poem is rather more than the simple description it first seems. A closer look at the syntax reveals that the three vignettes make a single sentence. This progressively builds up conditions for a fulfilment promised in the two closing lines, which are the sentence's long-awaited main clause.

Are the first two conditions (ll. 1 and 5) 'when' or 'if' clauses? German 'wenn' can mean either, but 'when' more obviously fits a sequence of times of day, especially after the opening adverb of time, '*Früh*, wenn...'. So: 'When the valley etc. emerge from the morning mists, then...'; 'When the sky...and when the east wind...'. The third condition (l. 9), on the other hand, is unambiguously an 'if' clause, introduced not by 'wenn' but by an inversion of subject and verb: 'dankst du' = wenn du dankst', 'If you give thanks'. We are thus waiting to hear both what happens 'when...', from sts. 1 and 2, and what will happen 'if...' from st. 3. It turns out that the answer is the same: 'there will be a glorious sunset'. Yet they were two quite different kinds of question. On the one hand, what sort of weather earlier in the day will lead to that kind of sunset? That is a matter of autumn weather patterns such as the poet had been observing. On the other hand, what sort of attitude in the observer will lead to that kind of sunset? A strange question surely, for human attitudes have no known meteorological effects. The poem is evidently talking on two different levels at once: literally about the serene end that is typical of fine autumn days, and not so literally about – what?

This is an old man's poem. He has seen many days and taken constant delight in watching natural phenomena unfold. All these occasions were a kind of imperceptible test of his responses: every 'when' was an ethical 'if'. The poem revisits two such, recent and as intensely felt as ever. Perhaps more intensely felt, because it is so late in life – 'sehnlich*st*em Erwarten' (superlatives are another stylistic thumbprint of the old Goethe). But these occasions were also, it is gently implied, representative of their like. The poem narrates them as phases in a real day; yet the day itself is also representative, perhaps suggesting the day of life. That does not make the poem allegorical, though. The perceptions have too much the feel of reality for that, and an even balance between real and representative makes symbol, not allegory.

We can perhaps trace how such symbolic meaning happens, as it (so to speak) creeps up on the poet unawares. Significantly, 'früh' in the opening line stands outside the three 'when'/'if' clauses, so it is a moment of real time recorded before any reflective structuring of experience began. The consequence is that, strictly speaking, 'früh' modifies all three, even 'wird vergolden' at the far end of the poem's single sentence and of the day it evokes – which is a contradiction of early and late. It looks as if the poem started with real perceptions in a real-time 'früh', and gradually slipped into reflection and the sense of a larger meaning. If this analysis is right, the unnoticed contradiction is a flaw to be cherished, a confirmation of Robert Frost's famous saying that 'a poem begins in beauty and ends in wisdom'.

lines 2 and 3: the datives are yet another unobtrusive means to compression; 'Nebelschleiern' instead of 'aus Nebelschleiern', and 'dem...Erwarten' instead of what would have had to be a full verb clause.

line 9: 'dich weidend' suggests, again, the intensity of pleasure.

line 10: 'Reiner Brust'. Structurally identical to 'Reiner Bahn' in the preceding poem, and placed at exactly the same point: the purity of the observed object must be matched by purity in the perceiving subject.

'der Großen, Holden'. The implied noun is surely 'Natur'; or conceivably 'Sonne' in the following line. For Goethe's 'sun-worship', see his very last recorded conversation with Eckermann, *Gespräche mit Goethe in den letzten Jahren seines Lebens*, 11 March 1832.

In ein Album   1831   **(p. 49)**
As a post-script to so many canonical poems, this graceful compliment from
an old man to a young woman is almost unknown. Yet it is a perfect example
of Goethe's late touch, effortlessly concise, conversationally relaxed. Indeed
the form 'würde...anvertrauen' in place of the subjunctive proper ('wenn...
anvertraute') is still strictly speaking frowned on! The seemingly casual 'wie
sie...' of ll. 2 and 3, however, echoes memorable phrases from the Bible about
the self-sufficient beauty of flowers: 'Sehet die Lilien auf dem Felde, wie sie
wachsen' (Matthew 6: 28) and 'Sehet die Lilien an, wie sie nicht spinnen
noch weben' (Luke 12: 27).